proclamation

6

Lessons

of the

Church Year

Ched Myers

PENTECOST 1

PROCLAMATION 6 | SERIES B

FORTRESS PRESS | MINNEAPOLIS

PROCLAMATION 6
Interpreting the Lessons of the Church Year
Series B, Pentecost 1

Scripture quotations, unless otherwise indicated, are from the New Revised Standard Version
Bible, copyright © 1989 by the Division of Christian Education of the National Council of
Churches in the U.S.A. and are used by permission.

Cover design: Ellen Maly
Text design: David Lott

The Library of Congress has cataloged the first four volumes of Series A as follows:

Proclamation 6, Series A: interpreting the lessons of the church
    year.
            p.   cm.
        Contents: [1] Advent/Christmas / J. Christiaan Beker — [2]
    Epiphany / Susan K. Hedahl — [3] Lent / Peter J. Gomes — [4] Holy
    Week / Robin Scroggs.
        ISBN 0-8006-4207-4 (v. 1 : alk. paper) — ISBN 0-8006-4208-2 (v.
    2 : alk. paper) — ISBN 0-8006-4209-0 (v. 3 : alk. paper) — ISBN 0-8006-4210-4
    (v. 4 : alk. paper).
        1. Bible—Homiletical use. 2. Bible—liturgical lessons,
    English.
    BS534.5P74   1995
    251—dc20   95-4622
                                                                   CIP
            Series B:
            Advent/Christmas / Arthur J. Dewey—ISBN 0-8006-4215-5
            Epiphany / Mark Allan Powell—ISBN 0-8006-4216-3
            Lent / James H. Harris, Jerome C. Ross, and Miles J. Jones—
                    ISBN 0-8006-4217-1
            Holy Week / Philip H. Pfatteicher—ISBN 0-8006-4218-X
            Easter / Beverly Roberts Gaventa—ISBN 0-8006-4219-8
            Pentecost 1 / Ched Myers—ISBN 0-8006-4220-1
            Pentecost 2 / Richard L. Eslinger—ISBN 0-8006-4221-X
            Pentecost 3 / Laura Lagerquist-Gottwald and Norman K. Gottwald—
                    ISBN 0-8006-4222-8

The paper used in this publication meets the minimum requirements of American National
Standard for Information Sciences—Permanence of Paper for Printed Library Materials,
ANSI Z329.48-1948.

Manufactured in the U. S. A.   AF 1-4220

00   99   98   97   96   1   2   3   4   5   6   7   8   9   10

Contents

In the fond memory of
Bartimaeus Community (1976–1984)
where I first learned the discipline
of preaching the lectionary

Preface

On the feast of Pentecost we renarrate the "birth" of the church in the power of the Holy Spirit. Yet what *sort* of practice the Spirit empowered at Pentecost, and continues to empower, has been a divisive issue in the life of the church ever since. Today the debate about what it means to be "Spirit-filled" usually focuses on individual charismatic gifts. The roots of Pentecost, however, are agricultural—and thus unavoidably *social* and *economic*.

Pentecost was a Jewish observance called the "Feast of Weeks" (*Shavuot*). Coming between Passover and the Feast of Tabernacles, *Shavuot* was originally a celebration of the first fruits of the harvest (Exod. 23:14-17; Deut. 16:9-12). However, after the Hellenistic period and the destruction of the Temple in 70 C.E., the festival became a commemoration of the giving of Torah to Moses on Mt. Sinai. This is how it continues to be celebrated in synagogue today.

There may be more to the symbolism of the original Feast of Weeks than harvest thanksgiving alone, however. It is interesting to note the similarity in calculations concerning the timing of the Levitical Feast of Weeks and that of the Jubilee:

> **Feast of Weeks:** From the day after the sabbath, from the day on which you bring the sheaf of the elevation offering, you shall count off seven weeks. . . . You shall count until the day after the seventh sabbath, fifty days; then you shall present an offering of new grain to the LORD. (Lev. 23:15)

> **Jubilee:** You shall count off seven weeks of years, seven times seven years, so that the period . . . gives forty-nine years. . . . And you shall hallow the fiftieth year and you shall proclaim liberty throughout the land to all its inhabitants. (Lev. 25:8,10)

This suggests that the feast of Pentecost was meant to remind Israel that "sabbath economics" applied at *each* harvest.

The word *sabbath* first appears in the Hebrew Bible in the Exodus story of manna in the wilderness (Exod. 16:23). This archetypal story was more than a lesson about God's sustaining love. It served as a reminder that the purpose of economic organization was for there to be enough for everyone, *not* for surplus accumulation that benefited the few (see Exod. 16:15-26 and 31:12-17). In this context Moses first prescribed periodic sabbath rest for both the land and human labor, an alternative rhythm that sought to disrupt human attempts to "control" the forces of production. Torah's sabbath regulations represented a strategy for teaching the people about their dependence upon the land and upon the divine economy of grace. The earth belongs to God, and its fruits are given to people as a gift (Lev. 25:23). Thus the people should freely and justly distribute those fruits, instead of seeking to own and hoard them.

Deuteronomy 15 extends sabbath logic: "Every seventh year you shall grant a remission of debts. . . . If a member of your community . . . is sold to you and works for you six years, in the seventh year you shall set that person free" (Deut. 15:1, 12). In agrarian societies such as biblical Israel (or parts of the Third World today), the cycle of poverty began when a family had to sell off its land in order to service a debt, and reached its conclusion when landless peasants could only sell their labor, becoming bond-slaves. Sabbath debt-remission was to be Israel's hedge against the inevitable tendency of human societies to concentrate power and wealth in the hands of the few and to create a class hierarchy with the poor at the bottom.

According to Leviticus 25, this cycle was supposed to culminate in a Jubilee, or "sabbath's sabbath" (for background on the Jubilee, see Ringe, 1985). The Jubilee sought to dismantle inequality through wealth redistribution,

- releasing each community member from debt (25:35-42);
- returning all encumbered or forfeited land to its original owners (vv. 13, 25-28);
- freeing all slaves (vv. 47-55).

The rationale for restructuring the community's assets, which includes a prohibition against lending money at interest (vv. 36f.), was to remind Israel of its identity as an exodus people who must never return to a system of slavery (v. 55).

The extent to which biblical Israel abided by the Jubilee code is a matter of much scholarly debate (and in capitalist religion, much skepticism). Yet sabbath economics remains at the heart of Torah—and of its feasts. It is significant, then, that Luke's narrative of Pentecost in Acts reappropriates the Jubilee implications of the Feast of Weeks. For when the Spirit descends, the redistribution of wealth and the "economics of enough" are once again realized (Acts 2:44-47; 4:32-37; see below, the second lesson for the Day of Pentecost). And as we will see in the Gospel lesson for the Second Sunday after Pentecost, Mark's Jesus sought to renew that old Jubilee vision in his practice as well.

It is to be expected that whenever God's Spirit is poured out on people, their traditions and institutions will be disrupted and disturbed. For in the great narrative of the Bible, God's intervention is always subversive.

YHWH is not a domesticated deity, baptizing our traditions and institutions, but One who seeks to liberate us from our enslaved condition, to heal us of our wounds and addictions, and to animate us in the practice of justice and compassion. The Acts narrative of Pentecost is not about ecstatic individual spiritual experience, but a challenge to the entire order of things, personal and political.

The same Spirit is just as subversive today. That is why my comments will emphasize these underappreciated socioeconomic themes as well as the more traditional theological dimensions of the lessons for the first ten weeks of Pentecost. My approach to the texts combines literary criticism, sociological exegesis, and political hermeneutics (on this see Myers, 1988:14ff.). I will consider each of the week's three lessons separately, and then will suggest themes for preaching the texts together (under *Homiletical Reflections*). Since there are a number of divergences between the four major lectionaries, I have chosen to follow the Revised Common Lectionary for most of my comments. I do, however, comment briefly on the other readings where they differ (under *Other Lessons*). On occasion I will recommend including more of a given text than is stipulated by the lectionary in order to honor the narrative integrity of a passage. I have used the New Revised Standard Version of the Bible except where indicated.

The challenge of the preacher is not only to help the community read the biblical texts of the day, but to be *read by* them. We live in a world where the problem of redistributing wealth and power represents the greatest challenge to the church's proclamation of "good news." May the texts in these early weeks of Pentecost inspire us to conspire with the Spirit to rise to this challenge.

Pentecost Sunday
The Day of Pentecost

Lectionary	First Lesson	Psalm	Second Lesson	Gospel
Revised Common	Acts 2:1-21 or Ezek. 37:1-14	Ps. 104:24-34, 35b	Rom. 8:22-27 or Acts 2:1-21	John 15:26-27; 16:4b-15
Episcopal (BCP)	Acts 2:1-11 or Isa. 44:1-8	Ps. 104:25-37 or 25-32 or 33:12-15, 18-22	1 Cor. 12:4-13 or Acts 2:1-11	John 20:19-23 or John 14:8-17
Roman Catholic	Acts 2:1-11	Ps. 104:1, 24, 29-31, 34	1 Cor. 12:3-7, 12-13	John 20:19-23
Lutheran (LBW)	Ezek. 37:1-14	Ps. 104: 25-34	Acts 2:1-21	John 7:37-39a

FIRST LESSON: EZEKIEL 37:1-14

The vision of the "valley of dry bones" is perhaps the best-known text in Ezekiel. Ezekiel's prophetic ministry spanned the first quarter of the sixth century B.C.E., before and during the Babylonian diaspora. This vision, addressed to weary exiles (37:11), is part of a series of oracles promising restoration for the nation. God's spirit breathing new life into old, dry bones (37:1-8) is portrayed in terms of "raising the dead" (37:9-13). This image was intended both as a consolation for those mourning real victims of the fall of Jerusalem as well as encouragement for a despairing and defeated people. But this oracle does more than affirm spiritual revival as a way of coping with the oppressive circumstances of exile; God also promises to "place you on your own soil" (37:14). In biblical faith, spiritual and material transformation are always linked.

The relationship of Ezekiel's vision to the Pentecost theme of "rebirth" through the Spirit is obvious. What is often overlooked, however, is the central role of the prophet in this revivification. Joseph Blenkinsopp suggests that Ezekiel may be alluding here to the story of the dead man who came back to life when he came into contact with Elisha's bones in 2 Kings 13:20f. (1983:203). Renewal is predicated upon the prophet's willingness to confront the profoundly alienated state of one's people ("they were very, very dry," 37:2).

Other Lessons: The oracle from Second Isaiah (44:1-8; *BCP*) also promises restoration. The intimacy of the relationship between God and Israel will be renewed as the Spirit is "poured out upon your descendants" (44:2-5). This theme is echoed by Joel (2:28), who is in turn cited by Peter in his Pentecost speech (Acts 2:17). The Isaiah text makes two allusions to the Song of Moses: Jacob as God's "darling" (cp. 44:2 and Deut. 32:15) and God as a "Rock" (cp. 44:8 and Deut. 32:4). The purpose of the people's renewal is to vindicate God's identity, to which they are "witnesses" (44:6-8).

SECOND LESSON: ACTS 2:1-21

Luke's story of the Spirit's descent on the disciples at Pentecost consists of three parts:

vv. 1-13	the experience of "tongues"
vv. 14-41	Peter's speech and the response of the crowd
vv. 42-47	the discipleship community of goods

The various lectionary lessons include less than half of this narrative, which is unfortunate since the three parts represent essential and interrelated characteristics of the nascent Christian movement portrayed here.

Robert Tannehill (1990:26) notes that the scene commences abruptly with the unusual phrase: "When the day of Pentecost was being fulfilled . . ." (v. 1). This may signal that the original intentions of the Feast of Weeks are about to be realized. The "first fruits" of the new messianic movement will be manifested publically while the Jubilee symbolism of Pentecost will be realized (see Preface). Indeed the narrative opens with "tongues of fire *distributed* among the disciples" (v. 3) and ends with them selling their possessions and "*distributing* them to whoever had need" (v. 45; the only two appearances of the Greek verb *diamerizō* in Acts). Peter's talk of the "gift" of the Spirit and the unilateral cancellation of debts in Jesus Christ (v. 38) echoes the Jubilee pronouncement of Jesus' first sermon (Luke 4:18ff.). All this suggests that Pentecost may have far more to do with the Jubilee vision of redistributory justice than with the ecstatic spectacle of glossolalia.

The setting of the story is also significant. The house in which the disciples are gathered (v. 2) is presumably the same place as the "upper room" of 1:13. As co-conspirators with someone who had just been executed as a political prisoner, the disciples are probably in hiding from the authorities. Whatever else the "great wind" of the Spirit did, it transformed fearful fugitives into "bold" public witnesses (v. 29). As Bill Kellermann points out, "The story in Acts 2 begins in the upper room and ends in the streets of Jerusalem. . . . After what's been done to Jesus, you'd have to be either crazy or drunk to be shouting his name in the streets and pointing accusing fingers at the executioners" (1991:200f.).

The "tongues as of fire" correlate to the baptism "with the Holy Spirit and with fire" promised by John the Baptist back in Luke 3:16 (see Acts

1:5). But these tongues are immediately put to practical use in vv. 4ff. We are told that witnessing this event are "devout Jews from every nation under heaven" (v. 5). From around the empire both Jews and Gentiles hear about the "powerful works of God" *in their own tongue* (v. 11). There is no indication that the tongues in this context are anything other than a symbol of cross-cultural communication. It is equally startling that these cosmopolitan visitors of high standing are being instructed by rural, uneducated, but suddenly polyglot Galileans (v. 7; see 4:13). Moreover, Luke has made it clear that women are part of the discipleship group (1:14), and Peter's argument from Joel confirms that *women* are participating in this prophetic revival (vv. 17f.). In other words, boundaries of race, class, and gender are being transgressed by a church empowered by the Spirit; a new "community without walls" is being born!

In order to interpret this remarkable event Peter cites the prophet Joel (Joel 2:28-32). The phrase "pouring out the spirit" there is notable because in most of the prophetic writings this verb (Heb. *shaphak*) is used in relation to God's wrath (e.g., Isa. 42:25; Jer. 6:11; Lam. 4:11; Ezek. 7:8; Hos. 5:10; Zeph. 3:8). Yet the judgment motif remains in the apocalyptic imagery of vv. 19f. The prophetic tradition that identifies divine intervention with cosmic upheaval (see, e.g., Isa. 13:9f.; 34:4; Ezek. 32:7; Amos 8:9; also Joel 2:10) is drawn upon heavily throughout the New Testament.

The judgment is made quite specific in the rest of Peter's speech (vv. 22-35; omitted by the lesson): It is the complicity of the nation as a whole in the execution of Jesus of Nazareth (vv. 23, 36). This indictment has been twisted to fuel millennia of Christian anti-Semitism, but can only be understood properly as a Jewish lament that the nation's leadership has once again chosen to silence rather than to heed a prophet, thereby forfeiting its legitimacy (a theme reiterated in later Acts speeches; see 3:22-26; 7:51f.). The exhortation to "save yourselves from this crooked generation" (v. 40) is an allusion to the ancient Song of Moses (Deut. 32:5).

Yet Jesus was more than a prophet: "Let all the house of Israel therefore know assuredly that God has made him both Lord and Messiah, this Jesus who you crucified" (v. 36). Peter could not have offered a more politically volatile conclusion. His people at that time were firmly under the boot of Caesar's "lordship," and all "messianic" movements were suspect by both the Roman and Judean authorities. Peter is, in other words, challenging the people to transfer their allegiance from executioner to victim (v. 38). The preaching of repentance will shortly land Peter in jail (Acts 4), just as it did his predecessors John the Baptist (Luke 3:8ff.) and Jesus of Nazareth (Luke 13:3-5).

Nor should we forget that behind Peter's critique of the public order is the alternative social practice of the Spirit-filled church (vv. 42-47). New converts are welcomed into a community in which "all things were held in common" (v. 44). By the end of the Pentecost narrative, the "house" has been transformed from a hiding place for fugitives (v. 2) to a place where Jubilee economics are celebrated at table (v. 46). Again we note how the Spirit's presence transforms human life inwardly and outwardly, privately and publically.

Other Lessons: The alternative *RCL* lesson is taken from Rom. 8:22-27. This text speaks of the "first fruits of the Spirit" (v. 23; Gk. *aparchē*), a harvest image from the Feast of Weeks. Paul elsewhere associates the first fruits with Israel (Rom. 11:16), with the resurrected Christ (1 Cor. 15:20, 23) and with Christian believers (Rom. 16:5; 1 Cor. 16:15). Here he is arguing that the "whole creation" is impatient to see the Christian community live into its vocation of liberation (vv. 21f.).

The notion of the Spirit empowering the equitable distribution of power and resources is stated another way in 1 Cor. 12:4-13 (Catholic, *BCP*). This is Paul's well-known metaphor of the church community as a "body," organically interrelated and interdependent. Diversity of gifts is affirmed (vv. 4f.), but the test of true Spirit-manifestation is clear: it must function "for the common good" (v. 7; Gk. *pros to sumpheron*). This term is used consistently in this epistle to warn the Corinthians that though within the economy of grace "all things may be lawful," all things do not necessarily benefit the community (6:12; 7:35; 10:23, 33). This principle undermines every attempt to turn charismatic power into elitism.

Paul's metaphor, perhaps adapted from Hellenistic political discourse, is reflexive: "Just as the body is one and has many members, so all the members of the body, though many, are one" (v. 12). It is the Spirit that unites, transforming ethnic ("Jews or Greeks") and class ("slaves or free") divisions into community (v. 13). This argument, reiterated in Gal. 3:27f., is one of the ways Paul appropriated the Jubilee ethic reflected in Acts. We will see him return to it in his discussion of economic sharing among Christian communities (see below, the Seventh Sunday after Pentecost).

GOSPEL: JOHN 7:37-39a; 14:8-17; 15:26f.; 16:4b-15; 20:19-23

The various readings from John's Gospel all deal with the Spirit as well. The RCL lesson focuses upon John's portrait of the Spirit as Advocate (15:26f.; 16:4b-15). This is no private, mystical relationship being proposed. The need for such a "true lawyer" (16:7, 13) arises from the concrete context of John's community, whose members are being dragged before hostile courts on charges of subversion (16:2). (This verse and 9:22

have been used to date John's Gospel in the late first century, since they appear to reflect the "Eighteen Benedictions," a document circulated declaring Christians unwelcome in the synagogue). Here the disciples must become "witnesses" (15:27; Gk. *marturion*, from which we derive our word *martyr*). Because only solidarity with the Trinitarian God can sustain such witness, John assures the disciples that because Jesus is "going to the Father," the Spirit will come (16:7).

The Advocate is not a defense lawyer, however, but a prosecutor who will seek to "convict" the world (16:8):

- of "sin" (16:9) because those who couldn't convict Jesus of sin still refuse to believe in him (see 8:45-47);
- of "justice" (16:10) because Judean courts will unjustly execute Jesus;
- and of "judgment" because the "ruler of this world" (14:30) will be overthrown by Jesus' death on the cross (see 12:31-33).

This offensive strategy in the face of official persecution functions to encourage Christian defendants to endure injustice because true justice will ultimately prevail. The Spirit is a reliable Advocate because she can "declare things to come" (16:13), an allusion to God's "case" against false authorities in Isaiah (Isa. 41:21-23).

The setting of the *LBW* lesson (7:37-39a) is the last day of the Feast of Tabernacles in Jerusalem. According to Wes Howard-Brook (1994:184ff.), it is just as the "priestly waters pour over the ceremonial altar" that Jesus stands up and invites the thirsty to come to him (v. 37). This may allude to another oracle of Second Isaiah that, interestingly, includes the promise of free food and drink for the penniless (Isa. 55:1). John 7:38, in turn, may be alluding to several Hebrew Bible traditions at once (e.g., Isa. 58:11; Prov. 5:15; Ps. 78:15f.; Ezek. 47:1-11), presenting Jesus as their fulfillment. The living waters will flow from the "belly," not the "heart" as in the RSV (Gk. *koilias*). The word was previously used by John in the context of Nicodemus's perplexity about whether "someone enter a second time into the mother's belly and be born" (3:4). Might the allusion in 7:38 even be to the water breaking before the delivery of a baby, thus strengthening the connection to "second birth"? Such a midwifing role for the Spirit (7:39) is certainly consistent with John's pneumatology.

The Catholic and *BCP* lesson (John 20:19-23) narrates Jesus' second appearance to the disciples in the Fourth Gospel, in which they receive the Holy Spirit (as in Acts, in a house). John is explicit that they were hiding out (v. 19), and Jesus attempts to calm their frayed nerves by twice offering them peace (vv. 20f.; the scene is repeated in v. 26). This peace is not that of the world (14:27), but a peace that empowers disciples to overcome the world (16:33). The point of the locked doors is not that Jesus walks through walls, but that he is able to transcend the fugitive disciples' fear in order to stand "in their midst." Howard-Brook points out that the showing of Jesus' "side and hands" was a symbolic state-ment, not a proof of his corporeality. No one can "snatch" disciples out of Jesus' *hands* (see 10:28). From his *side* blood and water flowed as a Roman spear confirmed his death (19:34), yet these elements are sym-bolic of new birth and true baptism (see 1 John 5:5-8). Thus at this moment of terror Jesus offers his disciples assurance that their political enemies will not prevail.

John's narrative of the gift of the Holy Spirit is considerably less spec-tacular than Luke's, but no less consequential (vv. 21f.). For the full authority of Jesus' "apostleship" ("sent by God"; see, e.g., 3:34; 5:36; 6:57; 8:42; 11:42; 17:8) is here transferred to the discipleship community (see 17:18). With this comes the Jubilary vocation of "releasing" people from sin/debt (v. 23). The alternate *BCP* lesson (14:8-17) turns to the first promise of the "Counselor" in John (vv. 16f.). This lesson echoes the same themes as those above: solidarity between disciples and the Trinitarian God (vv. 7-11); the empowerment of the disciples (v. 12); and the hostility of the world toward the "Spirit of Truth" (v. 17).

HOMILETICAL REFLECTIONS

On Pentecost it is appropriate to focus preaching on the Acts text and its presentation of the characteristics of a genuinely "Spirit-filled" church. The first lesson and Gospel support such a focus, and can be brought in throughout the sermon. "Can these bones live?" the prophet Ezekiel was asked by God while "in the spirit" (Ezek. 37:1-3). It is a question worth asking in our churches and in our culture today. The preacher's task is to "prophesy" in the valley of dry bones, not just to entertain parishioners with unoffensive stories. Peter's example at Pentecost shows how the Holy Spirit can "embolden" (2:29) someone who has known betrayal and dis-grace to speak the hard truth to his own people in order to bring about repentance and renewal (2:38ff.).

For Luke, the Spirit empowers the church to cross established (and enforced!) boundaries:

- of gender, as Peter endorses women prophets (Acts 2:17f.);
- of race, as the disciples engage in multilingual outreach to diaspora Jews and proselytes (2:9) and "all who are far off" (2:39); and

• of class, as "uneducated, common Galileans" preach to "devout leaders" (2:7) and even to the scribal authorities (4:13).

The Spirit-filled church crosses cultural and linguistic barriers in order to proclaim the good news (2:4-12); speaks hard truth to those who have acted unjustly and challenges them to repent (2:14-40); and embodies an alternative lifestyle of renewal and reconciliation (2:41-47). To what extent does this portrait characterize the church today?

"What does this mean?" (2:12)—indeed! It has often been pointed out that the "sign of tongues" foreshadows the pan-Mediterranean missionary reach of the gospel in Acts. What is overlooked, however, is the obvious: in this multilingual moment Luke is *affirming* the diverse cultural contexts in which the new Christian movement will spread. We might go further and say that Luke's Pentecost "tongues" story is a reiteration of the ancient tale of the Tower of Babel (Gen. 11:1-9). This Hebrew legend probably reflects a nomad's polemic against the powerful city-states of Mesopotamia, fiercely condemning the tower as a symbol of centralized power (Gen. 11:2); and idolatry (see Isa. 2:12-15). The imperial project of cultural conformity (Gen. 11:1, 6) is shattered and "dispersion" restored through linguistic diversity (Gen. 11:7f.; see Gen. 1:28; 9:1). The implication is that cultural hetereogeneity acts as a "natural" restraint upon the human impulse to construct societies of domination—a political insight that several millennia have only confirmed!

Luke's portrait of Pentecost renarrates Babel's lesson: "And at this sound the multitude came together and were confused because each one heard the apostles speaking in their own language" (Acts 2:6; the word for "confusion," Gk. *sungcheō*, is the same root word used in the Septuagint text of Gen. 11:7, 9). The point of the gift of tongues is to communicate the gospel across linguistic barriers, but not to eradicate those barriers. Unity through the Spirit does *not* mean speaking "one language"; instead there is an implied celebration of human diversity.

The issues of social architecture at stake in these biblical stories are still with us. *Human* variety is as essential to social ecology as species diversity is to a healthy biosystems, yet both are rapidly falling victim to global capitalism. The new Tower of Babel is the banal homogeneity of commercial culture and transnational technocracy. Christians in North America today who are suspicious of pluralism and who cling to the ideal of a dominant culture need to be reminded that the strongest biblical argument *for* diversity and *against* conformist centralism is also the oldest one. The church should renew this argument whenever it observes the Feast of Pentecost.

First Sunday after Pentecost
Trinity Sunday/Holy Trinity

Lectionary	First Lesson	Psalm	Second Lesson	Gospel
Revised Common	Isa. 6:1-8	Psalm 29	Rom. 8:12-17	John 3:1-17
Episcopal (BCP)	Exod. 3:1-16	Psalm 93	Rom. 8:12-17	John 3:1-16
Roman Catholic	Deut. 4:32-34, 39-40	Ps. 33:4-6, 9, 12, 18-20, 22	Rom. 8:14-17	Matt. 28:16-20
Lutheran (LBW)	Deut. 6:4-9	Psalm 149	Rom. 8:14-17	John 3:1-17

FIRST LESSON: ISAIAH 6:1-8

Isaiah's account of his call is dated during the year of king Uzziah's death (742 B.C.E.; v. 1a). Uzziah was the son of Amaziah and father of Jotham, all three of whom served as kings in Jerusalem during the eighth century (see 2 Chronicles 25–27). There may be irony in Isaiah's vision of the Temple (v. 1b), since Uzziah had been banned from there after contracting leprosy, which the Chronicler tells us was punishment for his attempt to usurp the role of the priests (2 Chron. 26:16-21).

Isaiah's Temple epiphany reminds Israel that YHWH transcends the Temple, which is filled by the hem of God's robe (v. 1). Only here in the Hebrew Bible do we meet *seraphim* (v. 2; *cherubim* appears ninety-one times). These "fiery ones" are possibly related to the fiery serpents of Num. 21:6-9 (*saraphim*; see also Ezek. 1:27). The quaking, smoke-filled house (v. 4) brings to mind both the cloud that surrounded Mt. Sinai (Exod. 19:16-19). The imagery of fire here probably means to allude to the burning bush of Exodus 3, where God is revealed as the "self-naming One" (below, *Other Lessons*). Here the *seraphim* emphatically announce God's "holiness" (v. 3). "Fire is one of the central motifs in ancient Israel for conveying the danger that exists when the holy God enters the profane world," writes Thomas Dozeman (1993:22). "Fire is so often associated with the holy because it is two-sided and hence dangerous: It can destroy or purify." According to the pollution code of ancient Israel, a person must die after beholding the holiness of God (v. 5; see Exod. 33:20; Judg. 13:22). But Isaiah is spared by the *seraphim*, who purge his "unclean lips" with an ember from the altar (v. 6f.).

The commissioning of Isaiah begins not with a divine command, as is elsewhere the case with Hebrew prophets, but with a divine plea (v. 8a). In contrast to the resistance to God's call by Moses (Exod. 4:10) and Jeremiah (Jer. 1:4-8), Isaiah "volunteers" for the job (v. 8b). Though his marching orders are not included as part of the lesson, they should be, since they represent the heart of the story (vv. 9f.). This harsh oracle about eyes that do not see and ears that do not hear represents a "reality check" for the eager apostle. Isaiah is warned that the more he speaks the truth to his people, the less inclined they will be to accept his message. The reason is simple: if people acknowledge their error they must change their way of life (v. 10b). It is *repentance* they refuse, choosing illusions of innocence instead. This powerful portrait of human resistance to the Word of God is cited by Mark in Jesus' parables sermon (Mark 4:10-12), and he adopts Isaiah's indictment of "blind eyes, deaf ears and a dull mind" as his master metaphor for the pathology of denial (Mark 8:17f.). Isaiah understandably despairs that his work will thus be futile: "How long, O Lord?" (v. 11a). The answer is grim: until the devastating consequences of denial run their course, which will include collapse and deportation (vv. 11b-13). No matter how bad things get, however, there will always be a remnant for renewal, called the "holy seed" (6:13c). This image may have been an inspiration for Jesus' sower parable (Mark 4:3-9).

Other Lessons: The *LBW* lesson is the great commandment of Torah, the *Shema*: "Hear, O Israel: The LORD our God is one" (Deut. 6:4). This might seem at first a strange text to read on *Trinity* Sunday, but is appropriate because it takes us to the roots of the biblical confessional tradition. As Thomas Mann puts it, "The *Shema* empasizes that the total person—and the total community—must pledge its allegiance to Yahweh, and to no other" (1988:150). For the Jewish people *Shema* (from the first word "Hear!") is not only spoken (vv. 6f.), but *worn* (v. 8; see Exod. 13:9, 16). In our world of conflicting loyalties, we Christians would do well to learn the *Shema* by heart as well.

The Catholic lesson sounds a similar note with a series of rhetorical questions posed by Moses to Israel concerning the unique character of God (Deut. 4:32-34, 39f.). One of them echoes the Isaiah lesson: "Has any people ever heard the voice of a god speaking out of a fire, as you have heard, and lived?" (v. 33). These queries are meant to get the people to acknowledge the fundamental tenant of radical monotheism: "The LORD is God in heaven above and on the earth below; there is no other" (v. 39).

The *BCP* lesson (Exod. 3:1-16) returns us to the foundational biblical epiphany: Moses and the burning bush. Like the Isaiah lesson, this story includes images of fire (vv. 2f.), holiness (v. 5), and the prophet's terror at God's presence (v 6b). It represents the defining moment in biblical history for two reasons. First, God is revealed clearly as the One who hears the cry of the oppressed and who animates a movement of liberation: "I have observed the misery of my people who are in Egypt. . . . I know their sufferings, and I have come down to deliver them" (vv. 7f.). Not only did this revelation launch the great narrative of Israel's exodus, but as Michael Walzer (1986) has shown, it has continued to inspire social movements for freedom and justice ever since, including our contemporary theologies of liberation.

Second, this text is definitive because it narrates God's self-naming. Moses, in the first of three attempts to avoid his commission (see 4:1, 10), poses a revealing double question to the Voice from the bush: "Who am *I* that I should go to Pharaoh?" (v. 11); and "Who shall I tell the Israelites *you* are?" (v. 13). To Moses' first protest comes the answer, "I will be with you" (v. 12), a reiteration of God's promise to Jacob (Gen. 28:15). In tension with this assurance of accompaniment, however, is the response to Moses' second query, which asserts God's radical autonomy (v. 14). "I will be who I will be" is captured in the great tetragrammaton YHWH (v. 15). The God of Abraham, Isaac, and Jacob (v. 6) is free, unnamable and undomesticated—that is why YHWH animates liberation among us.

SECOND LESSON: ROMANS 8:12-17

This passage, set in the context of Paul's exposition of the believer's life under grace (Romans 5–8), is no doubt chosen for Trinity Sunday because of its invocation of the "Abba, Father" (v. 15b), the Christ (v. 17), and the Spirit (vv. 13f., 16). Paul's description of the struggle between "spirit" and "flesh" (vv. 12f.) must not be interpreted in terms of Neoplatonic dualism, which concerns itself with escape from corporeal existence into some ideal spiritual world. Rather, it represents the conflict between two "domains" that characterizes apocalyptic perception: the domain of freedom and the domain of bondage (for background on Paul's use of apocalyptic, see Beker, 1982). These domains (also called "grace" and "sin" by Paul) compete for the minds and hearts of the community and of individuals in the world.

Paul understands this struggle as a kind of existential renarration of the Exodus story. The condition of bondage ("living according to the flesh") is equated with indebtedness (v. 12), to which the whole of creation is held hostage (see vv. 20f.). But insofar as Christians are "led by the Spirit"(v. 14), as Israel was led through the wilderness by an angel (Exod. 23:20), we too can inherit the designation "children" (beginning in Exod. 1:9 the Hebrews are referred to as the "children of Israel" throughout the rest of the Torah). For the people of God were not created to live under the Egyptian condition, the "spirit of slavery" (v. 15). Our "adoption" as children is confirmed by the privilege of addressing God intimately as "Abba" (the Aramaic word for "daddy"; see Mark 14:36). Paul spells this idea out further in Gal. 4:1-7. He consistently stipulates one condition of this magnificent new status, however: "Provided that we suffer with Christ in order that we may also be glorified with him" (v. 17).

GOSPEL: JOHN 3:1-17

The Gospel lesson is the famous story of Nicodemus. According to Wes Howard-Brook (1994:20ff.), the Fourth Gospel reflects a period in the late first century C.E. in which John's community had been expelled from the synagogue and was suffering persecution from both Roman and Judean authorities. In the highly symbolic world of Johannine narrative, Nicodemus is portrayed negatively:

- "There was a man": according to 2:24f., Jesus "knows men" and does not need their witness;
- "of the Pharisees . . . a ruler of the Judeans": the Pharisees are opponents (7:32ff.), while the "rulers" will seek to kill Jesus (7:25f.);
- "came to Jesus by night": a symbol of the darkness in John (9:4; 11:10);
- believes Jesus' "signs": Jesus does not "trust himself" to those who believe because of signs alone (2:23f.).

This explains why Nicodemus must change radically if he wishes to see the "kingdom of God" (v. 3; this image, so common in the Synoptics, occurs only here in John).

The phrase to be "born again," so dear to contemporary evangelical Christians, carries a specific connotation in Johannine narrative: the public commitment of Christian baptism. This Jesus makes clear in v. 5, which may also allude to Ezekiel's image of the renewal of Israel by "water and spirit" (Ezek. 36:25ff.). John underlines the baptismal context with his use of "flesh and spirit" (vv. 6f.), the same apocalyptic dualism we saw in the Romans passage above. The Spirit/wind cannot be managed by authorities such as Nicodemus; it "blows where it will" (v. 8).

Nicodemus, trying to keep this encounter covert, first is baffled (v. 4), then protests (v. 9). This earns him a sharp rebuke from Jesus (v. 10), consistent with the Johannine community's criticism of its synagogue rivals. This community complains that "you do not receive our testimony" (v. 11). The polemic then moves to John's favorite tactic: contrasting the authority of Jesus to that of Moses (vv. 12-16; see 1:17; 5:45f; 6:32; 7:23; 9:28f.).

While Moses may have "ascended" Mt. Sinai (Exod. 19:20), the "Human One descended from heaven" (v. 13; see Bar. 3:29). Moses may have "lifted up" the serpent to allow Israel to "live" (Num. 21:9), but Jesus himself will be "lifted up" and thus offer "eternal life" (vv. 14f.; the first of seventeen occurrences of this phrase in John). This is the first of three times Jesus speaks of being "lifted up" on the cross in John (see 8:28; 12:32-34), paralleling the three passion portents in the Synoptic Gospels. The lesson closes with the famous text of John 3:16, the thesis statement of the Gospel. It emphasizes that despite John's severe criticism of "the world" in this story, God's aim is to redeem it.

Other Lesson: The Catholic lesson is the concluding lines of Matthew's Gospel, also chosen because of the Trinitarian formula of the Great Commission (Matt. 28:19). The disciples ascend a mountain in Mosaic fashion and there see the resurrected Jesus (vv. 16f.). Jesus' announcement that "all authority in heaven and on earth has been given to me" undergirds the universal mission ("to all nations") of the church (vv. 18-20).

HOMILETICAL REFLECTIONS

Trinity Sunday invites us to consider the unique character of the biblical God. Any of the first lessons, as "foundational" texts of the Hebrew Bible, provide a good starting point. The *Shema*, the burning bush, and the Temple vision of Isaiah all attest to a God who is emphatically *not* a product of human manufacture. In trying to find a modern analogy for the ancient notion of holiness many contemporary theologians have rightly spoken of the radical "otherness" of God. YHWH is not a philosophic concept, nor a projection of our superego, nor a patron of our national aspirations, nor a *deus ex machina*, nor a cosmic engineer, nor any of the other ways that philosophers and politicians have "named" God. God is self-naming. Unconstrained by nature or history, God is free to bring us hope from outside both. This is the heart of biblical—and Trinitarian—faith.

"And the hem of God's robe filled the temple" (Isa. 6:1). Isaiah's vision belittles our cultic attempts to "house" the Presence. The great Temple of Solomon, despite its grandeur, couldn't contain even the trailing end of YHWH's outer garment. Trinity Sunday is a good time to remind ourselves that God can never "fit" in our churches. So it is both pedagogically and theologically appropriate that our liturgies have adopted the refrain of Isaiah's seraphim: "Holy, Holy, Holy."

But what of the God who is "Three-in-One"? The preacher would do well to avoid theological treatise and concentrate on images, as the lessons do. My pastor introduced me to a delightful metaphor for the Trinity in her sermon on this feast a few years ago. It seems that John of Damascus, an eighth-century theologian, proposed the idea of an exchange of energy between the persons of the Trinity using the Greek word *perichoresis*, which comes from the same root as the word *choreography*. My pastor invited us to imagine the Godhead as a perpetual circle dance, from which the dance of life flows in endless choreography.

But before we get too carried away with speculative metaphors, let us remember that the theme that runs through most of today's lessons is *conversion*, not God-talk. Isaiah's enthusiasm for mission must be tempered by the divine reminder that his call to "turn around" will not be welcomed (Isa. 6:10). John relates "an archetypal encounter challenging a person powerful in the eyes of the world to convert and become powerful in the eyes of God" (Howard-Brook: 87). And Paul reminds us that conversion is the constant struggle to live according to the "Spirit," not the flesh.

Perhaps we can learn something from the practical "theology" of the Twelve Step program. The road to sobriety begins with "conversion," understood in terms of apocalyptic dualism: the addict is either in denial or in recovery. Twelve Step discourse acknowledges that recovery is impossible without help from "outside" oneself, yet little energy is spent trying to define the "Higher Power." The focus is instead upon the daily struggle for sobriety. The otherness of God invites us to be similarly discontinuous with business-as-usual.

From the lessons we can sketch a portrait of the Trinity who both demands and empowers this kind of conversion. In Isaiah, God-the-Parent calls for apostles to speak hard truth to a people in denial. John's Gospel portrays Jesus as such an apostle, confronting the powerful with the challenge of new birth. And Paul speaks of God-the-Spirit who midwifes the birth of new "children."

Second Sunday after Pentecost
Ninth Sunday in Ordinary Time
Proper 4

Lectionary	First Lesson	Psalm	Second Lesson	Gospel
Revised Common	I Sam. 3:1-10 (11-20 *or* Deut. 5:12-15	Ps. 139:1-6, 13-18 *or* Ps. 81:1-10	2 Cor. 4:5-12	Mark 2:23—3:6
Episcopal (BCP)	Deut. 5:6-21	Psalm 81 *or* Ps. 81:1-10	2 Cor. 4:5-12	Mark 2:23-28
Roman Catholic	Deut. 5:12-15	Ps. 81:2-8, 10-11	2 Cor. 4:6-11	Mark 2:23-28 *or* Mark 2:23—3:6
Lutheran (LBW)	Deut. 5:12-15	Ps. 81:1-10	2 Cor. 4:5-12	Mark 2:23-28

FIRST LESSON: I SAMUEL 3:1-20

This week begins Ordinary Time (Proper 4 for Anglo-Catholics). For the rest of the period covered in this book, the first lesson in the RCL will be taken from First and Second Samuel. The other lectionaries skip around the Hebrew Bible.

As did last week's lesson, 1 Samuel 3 narrates a call story, this time of the prophet and judge Samuel. It is preceded by the story of the birth of Samuel (1:1-20) and the Song of Hannah (2:1-10), upon which the evangelist Luke draws in his nativity scenes (Luke 1). Hannah's celebration of God's power to overturn the social order ("The bows of the mighty are broken, but the feeble gird on strength," 2:4) will be a theme throughout the Samuel narrative. The first object lesson is the decline of the priestly household of Eli, which oversaw the cultic "house" at Shiloh (2:12ff.). By the end of chap. 3 Samuel has eclipsed Eli as the prophet through whom God speaks (3:19-21).

The story of the transition plays off Eli's poor "sight" and Samuel's defective "hearing" (vv. 2-8). In classic threefold fashion the altarboy Samuel mistakes the call of God for that of the old priest, who must tutor him in how to respond (v. 9). Ironically, the message to Samuel seals the doom of Eli (vv. 10-14). Once again we see that the fearful job of the prophet is to speak hard truth to those in power (vv. 15-17). But Eli humbly accepts the judgment (v. 18). Chapter 4 then narrates Israel's defeat at the hands of the Philistines, in which Eli's wayward sons are killed and the ark captured, at which news Eli himself dies (4:10-18).

The point of the lesson is not so much the ascendancy of Samuel as the downfall of Eli because of corruption. Just as Eli's offspring used their

position for exploitation and gain (2:12-17), next week's lesson will show
that the same thing happened to Samuel's offspring (8:1-3). This is the thesis that shapes all the "historical" narratives of the Hebrew Bible: personal
and political disasters are *always* first the result of injustice within the
community, not external threat.

Other Lesson: The *BCP* lesson continues its series of foundational texts
from the Hebrew Bible, in this case the Ten Commandments (Deut. 5:6-
21). The *LBW* and Catholic lessons focus only on the injunction to "keep
the sabbath holy" (vv. 12-15), in which we see the one major difference
between the Deuteronomic Decalogue and that of Exod. 20:2-17. In Exodus the rationale for the sabbath is the order of creation (Exod. 20:11),
while here it is a reminder of Israel's liberation from slavery in Egypt
(Deut. 5:15; see v. 6). This focus on the sabbath and liberation resonates
with today's Gospel lesson.

SECOND LESSON: 2 CORINTHIANS 4:5-12

This Sunday begins six weeks in Paul's "second" letter to the the Christians at Corinth. This epistle likely preserves more than one correspondence. Victor Paul Furnish believes that 2 Corinthians 1–9 and 10–13 represent Paul's fourth and fifth letters to the Corinthian church respectively, 1
Corinthians being the second and the first and third letters having been lost
(1984:29ff.). The lesson is from a section in which Paul asserts his apostolic credentials (2:14—5:19), distinguishing himself from "hucksters of
the word of God" (2:17) and those who "pride themselves on position"
(5:12). Throughout the epistle Paul seeks to "prove" his apostleship in
terms of marginalization rather than status, suffering rather than self-
advancement, and grace rather than merit.

Paul begins this part of his argument by stipulating that his service (Gk.
diakonian) is a response to the mercy of God, unlike those Christian teach-
ers who "walk in ways" (a Pauline metaphor for lifestyle) that are under-
handed and fraudulent (4:1f.). Paul believes it is impossible to recognize
the sovereignty of Christ while promoting one's self-interest (v. 5). Only
here does he propose himself as a "slave" of the community of faith, rather
than of Christ. Paul's freedom to serve stands in sharp contrast to those
who, as he writes later, "make slaves of you, or prey upon you, or take
advantage of you" (11:20).

While "the god of this world has blinded the mind of unbelievers to
keep them from seeing the light" (v. 4), Paul's enlightenment comes from
"the God who said, 'Let there be light'" (v. 6; see Isa. 9:2). This God has

been revealed "in the face of Christ" (more than in the "face of Moses," 3:7). Yet the infinite value of this "treasure" is entrusted to humans who, like "earthen vessels," are fragile and common (v. 7). This confirms one of Paul's favorite themes: divine, not human, strength animates his work (see 3:5; 12:9; 13:4).

Apparently the Corinthian church, not unlike the North American church today, was impressed with the displays of charismatic power by those who preached a theology of aggrandizement. Against this prestige-oriented Christianity Paul pits his own commitment to discipleship (vv. 8-11). He catalogues the realities of following Jesus in four antitheses:

- *in all things afflicted, but not constricted*: this probably refers to Paul's refusal to constrain his own activites despite their danger (see 1:4; 7:5);
- *desperate but never in total despair*: Paul has already alluded to a "near death" situation in 1:8f., probably imprisonment in Ephesus with possibility of execution (reflected in Phil. 1:19ff. and 2:17?).
- *persecuted but not forsaken*: this may be an oblique reference to the Colosseum games (see 1 Cor. 4:9-13), and/or to Paul's isolation because of the political risk he represented;
- *struck down but not destroyed*: perhaps reference to the many beatings Paul endured (see 11:23ff.).

Paul's list is not merely rhetorical, for it alludes to actual political persecution he has endured at the hands of both Jewish and Roman authorities. As Furnish points out, though his Stoic contemporaries used similar language, Paul sees hardship not as a discipline that engenders greater detachment, but as the price of fidelity (ibid: 283ff.).

The passage concludes with a remarkable meditation about living and dying for and with Jesus (vv. 10-12). The above litany represents the rule, not the exception, for the apostlic vocation ("We *always* carry about . . ."; see 1 Cor. 15:30f.). If v. 10 refers to an existential kind of dying (Gk. *nekros*), being "handed over to death" refers to political execution, as in the Gospels (v. 11; Gk. *thanatos*; see Mark 1:14; 9:31; 13:9; also Acts 3:13; 22:4; 28:17; Rom. 4:25). There are, in fact, some interesting parallels in this lesson with some of Jesus' exhortations recorded in the Synoptic tradition:

Paul: as your *slaves*. (v. 5)
Jesus: Whoever would be first among you must be *slave* of all. (Mark 10:44)
Paul: We are always being *handed over* to death *for Jesus' sake*, so that the life of Jesus may be manifested in our flesh. (v. 11)
Jesus: Whoever loses their life *for my sake* and the gospel's will save it (Mark 8:35). They will *hand you over . . . for my sake*. . . . (Mark 13:9)

Is Paul here echoing this discipleship tradition? It is significant that of the seventeen times he uses "Jesus" (vs. his more normal "Christ"), *seven* occur in 2 Cor. 4:5-14! In any case, Paul is arguing that true solidarity with Jesus is to be found not in ecstatic spiritual experiences or charismatic miracle-working but in "renarrating" the story of the Nazarene in one's own life and death (see below, the Seventh Sunday after Pentecost).

GOSPEL: MARK 2:23—3:6

Epiphany occasioned lessons from the first chapter of Mark, the Gospel for Year B, but it is used sparingly during Lent and Easter. Ordinary Time now picks up Mark's narrative in the middle of a conflict sequence from Jesus' first "campaign" in and around Capernaum. Jesus has challenged the purity code by "declaring clean" a leper, expropriating the authority of the priestly caste (1:40-45). He then took on the debt system, similarly undermining the scribal "franchise" by unilaterally declaring debt-forgiveness (2:1-12). Jesus next tangles with the Pharisees (2:15ff.).

During the period of late Second Temple Judaism the clerical aristocracy tended to take an elitist attitude toward purity and debt regulations. They did not expect the masses to keep all the laws; such piety was for the educated and the affluent. In contrast the Pharisaic sect, a Jewish renewal movement that was rapidly gaining social power and influence in Mark's time, sought to extend the scope of purity and debt through a program that encouraged popular piety relevant to daily village life.

Like the Jesus movement, then, the Pharisees were critical of the ruling Judean elite. They threatened the priests because they gave more emphasis to practical, local obligations (particularly agricultural and household matters) than to Temple-centered ones. They threatened the scribes as professional interpreters of Torah because they contended that an "oral Torah" was also given to Moses on Sinai and handed down over the centuries through rabbinic teaching. It is testimony to the genius of Pharisaism that after the destruction of the Jerusalem Temple in 70 c.e. it emerged as the dominant group within Judaism, laying the groundwork for a synagogue-based faith and practice.

With different visions for renewal, Christians and Pharisees competed for the hearts and minds of the people. Mark 2:15-28 portrays Pharisaic preoccupation with the dietary, ritual, and legal issues surrounding proprietary table fellowship. A series of controversies concerning *with whom one eats* (vv. 15-17) and *when one should refrain from eating* (vv. 18-22) culminates in today's lesson, a story about *where and when one should eat* (vv. 23-28). As in the other two episodes, Jesus' disciples draw fire from the Pharisees, this time for cutting through a field and stripping grain to eat (vv. 23f.).

The Pharisees' complaint is based upon Sabbath restrictions regarding harvesting. Jesus' defense appeals to a somewhat loose rendering of a scriptural story about David (v. 25; see 1 Sam. 21:1-6). As a guerilla fighter on campaign David "commandeered" the bread of the Presence for his soldiers, violating the holiness code because he was in "need." But Mark has added something to the story: David and his followers were *hungry*. This story endorses the Jubilee notion that hungry people have a right to food *despite* laws that restrict such access (see the Preface). It resonates with at least two Levitical principles:

> If any of your kin fall into difficulty and become dependent on you, you shall support them. . . . You shall not lend them your money at interest or provide them food at a profit. (Lev. 25:35, 37)

> When you gather the harvest in your country, you are not to gather the gleanings. . . . Leave them to the poor and the stranger. (Lev. 23:22)

Some historical background about problems of economic justice in Mark's time clarifies why these issues arise in relation to the Pharisees.

The settings of these controversy stories represent the "economic sphere" of a traditional agricultural society: the *table* was the primary site of "consumption," the *field* of "production." In the late Second Temple period there was resentment among Galilean peasants about the control exercised by the Pharisaic establishment over the sowing, harvesting, and marketing of produce. Many poor peasants could not afford to obey laws concerning tithing, or leaving their fields fallow during the sabbath year, or what they should and shouldn't plant or eat. From their point of view, the Pharisees' adjudication of sabbath rules had become a way of regulating the economy to Pharisaic benefit.

Mark's grainfield action narrates nothing less than civil disobedience, advocating "food for people, not for profit." How else are we to interpret Jesus' dictum that "the sabbath should be at the service of humanity, not vice versa" (v. 27)? Later in Mark's narrative "bread" (v. 26) will be revealed as a symbol of community sharing in the manna/Jubilee tradition (6:33-44; see below, the Ninth Sunday of Pentecost). Matthew, the first interpreter of Mark, certainly understood the point of Mark's story here to be the priority of justice (see Matt. 12:1-8).

The grainfield action sets the stage for the climax to Jesus' Capernaum campaign in another Sabbath controversy (3:1-6; omitted by the *LBW* and *BCP* lessons). We are returned to the heart of the symbolic order—synagogue on a Sabbath—where the campaign began in 1:21. The Pharisees' complaint in v. 24 is a kind of legal warning after which charges will be pressed. Jesus' summary "overruling" of this accusation in v. 28 thus ensures that the conflict will escalate.

This episode is determined political theater, a showdown between Jesus' mission to restore the Jubilee and the ideological imperatives of the dominant order. It is a kind of trial scene: in the public glare of media lights the authorities stand poised, ready for him to "cross the line" (3:2). But Jesus suddenly turns from defendant to prosecutor. His challenge seems at first to be a rhetorical question: "Is it against the law on the sabbath day to do good or evil?" (3:4). He then adds wryly, "To save life or to kill?" as if to contrast his own healing ministry with the authorities' concern for state security (see 8:31; 14:1). But this is no rhetorical question. It is a para-phrase of the great ultimatum given by Moses to the people of Israel who stood on the boundary of the Promised Land:

> See, I have set before you today life and prosperity, death and adversity. If you obey the commandments of God. . . . then you shall live. . . . But if your heart turns away and you do not hear . . . you shall perish. (Deut. 30:15-18)

This timeless moment composed by the Deuteronomist suspends the peo-ple between "heaven and earth," between history and destiny, between ancestors and descendants. It is an existential moment that invites the read-er into its archetypal choice between life and death.

But Jesus' audience refuses to answer. The word describing his fury in 3:5 is a strong one, usually reserved in the New Testament for "the wrath of God." Mark indicts their obstinance as "hardness of heart"—"Pharaoh's disease" in the Exodus tradition (see also Deut. 29:4; 29:18; 30:1, 6). This charge will later be leveled against Jesus' own disciples as well (6:52; 8:17). It is a watershed moment. Jesus, choosing life, heals the disabled man. In the classic tradition of civil disobedience, he breaks the law in order to raise deeper issues about the moral health of the common life. The Galilean officials, meanwhile, choose death, launching their plot against Jesus (3:6). From here on these two trajectories will define Mark's narra-tive, as Jesus continues his healing work against growing opposition from the authorities.

HOMILETICAL REFLECTIONS

The lessons remind us that corruption is endemic in human society. Eli's sons, the Pharisees of the Gospel, and the "apostles of self-interest" criti-cized by Paul, all demonstrate that some people will exploit their positions for gain. It is this phenomenon of inevitable inequality that the Jubilee sought to address by proposing a regular "corrective" redistribution of wealth and power.

Mark's series of eating controversies with the Pharisees seeks to renew this Jubilee vision against the backdrop of the politics of food in agrarian Palestine. In the first episode, debtors and repentant debt-collectors are pictured together at table fellowship (2:15f.). The second episode critiques the ritual piety of fasting in a world of real hunger, and counterproposes banquet abundance as a better symbol of holiness (2:19f.). And today's Gospel lesson dramatizes an object lesson in Jubilee in a local grainfield. The clinching argument is that the Human One is sovereign over the sabbath (2:28), just as he is over the debt system (2:10). This pronouncement suggests that the whole sequence, beginning with 2:1, is a radical reinterpretation of the debt code in light of Jubilee. Reenacting the Mosaic ultimatum, Jesus then poses the question of what it means to be a sabbath people in 3:4. It is a query that affluent Christian churches in North America would do well to ponder.

Mark's is a story of political realism: scarcely one-fifth of the way through the book Jesus is already marked for death. Jubilee practice may invoke the divine economy of grace, but it is, as Bonhoeffer reminds us, "costly grace." Such economic practice and its political cost are understood perfectly by the apostle Paul. In our world of criminal concentrations of wealth and power, are we willing to follow Jesus into the "fields of economic oppression" (Mark 2:23), so that "the life of Jesus might be manifested in our bodies" (2 Cor. 4:11)?

Third Sunday after Pentecost
Tenth Sunday in Ordinary Time
Proper 5

Lectionary	First Lesson	Psalm	Second Lesson	Gospel
Revised Common	I Sam. 8:4-11, (12-15), 16-20, (11:14-15) or Gen. 3:8-15	Psalm 138 or 130	2 Cor. 4:13—5:1	Mark 3:20-35
Episcopal (BCP)	Gen. 3:(1-7), 8-21	Psalm 130	2 Cor. 4:13-18	Mark 3:20-35
Roman Catholic	Gen. 3:9-15	Ps. 130:1-8	2 Cor. 4:13—5:1	Mark 3:20-35
Lutheran (LBW)	Gen. 3:9-15	Ps. 61:1-5, 8	2 Cor. 4:13-18	Mark 3:20-35

FIRST LESSON: I SAMUEL 8:4-20

This lesson narrates one of the fatal turning points in Israel's history: the ascendency of a king. According to the book of Joshua, the ideal form of "government" among the Israelite tribes in the promised land was a kind of decentralized confederacy. Each tribe was to administer their own affairs under the leadership of local political-military "judges" (such as we saw in Eli and Samuel in last week's lesson). The twelve tribes were to be unified by their covenant with God. As narrated in the book of Judges, whenever the tribes abandoned this model, they could no longer resist assimilation into Canaanite society, and would fall into idolatry and lose their freedom (Judges 2). Then God would again "raise up judges who delivered them out of the power of those who plundered them" (Judg. 2:16).

The theological notion that YHWH was king over Israel is reflected in some of the enthronement Psalms (e.g. Pss. 29:1, 10; 93:1-4; 95:3; 96:10; 99:1, 4). But whereas normally in the ancient Near East the royalty of the deity *mirrored and legitimated* the role of the tribal king, the earlier Hebrew traditions insist that God's sovereignty *precluded* the political form of kingship. Judges 8:22f., for example, reports that the victorious Israelite military leader Gideon rejected the peoples' offer to make him king: "I will not rule over you. . . . YHWH will rule over you." Instead, Gideon left decision-making up to "seventy sons" (Judg. 8:29-32). But one of these sons, Abimelech, launched a coup in alliance with the "lords of Shechem," which slaughtered his kin to grab sole power (9:1-6). This inspired the sole remaining son, Jotham, to spin his anti-kingship parable of the trees (9:7-15), which became inspiration for later political parables in the biblical tradition (see below, the Fourth Sunday after Pentecost).

Norman Gottwald contends that the early Israelite "intertribal protective association" represented a revolutionary alternative to the dominating, centralized rule of Cannaanite city-states (1985:284ff.). He describes its social organization as essentially egalitarian. The refrain in Judges is, "In those days there was no king in Israel" (Judg. 17:6; 18:1; 19:1; 21:25). But this experiment of self-determination did not last. The first part of 1 Samuel describes the collapse of the system of Judges, which, as we saw in last week's lesson, is attributed more to internal corruption than to the military threat of the Philistines (1 Samuel 4). According to Gottwald it was the development of "imbalances in wealth and lapses in the tribal mutual aid system" that led to certain powerful "houses" (such as those of Saul and David) to compete for power (ibid: 319ff.). This in turn led inexorably to the establishment of a more conventional, centralized monarchy under David, and then to a full-blown Temple-state under Solomon. The long-term result was not stability but civil war, disastrous external political alliances, and finally conquest and exile.

Even during the Israelite monarchy the suspicion of state authority survived, most visible in this week's lesson. 1 Samuel 7 narrates the last great "moment" of the old system in which Samuel operates as both military leader and "circuit judge." But 8:1-3 reports that "his sons did not follow in his ways, but turned aside after gain; they took bribes and perverted justice." The tribal leaders, understandably disillusioned with such corruption, call for a more conventional political arrangement: "Appoint for us a king to govern us, like other nations" (vv. 4f.).

God consoles Samuel's despair: "They have not rejected you; they have rejected me from being king over them" (v. 7). But God instructs him to warn the people about "the ways of the king who shall reign over them" (v. 9). The catalogue is instructive. With a monarchy will come:

- forced conscription (v. 11);
- a standing army and a militarized economy (v. 12);
- State expropriation of labor and resources (vv. 13, 16);
- an economy geared to the elite (v. 14); and of course,
- heavy taxation (vv. 15, 17).

This grim litany concludes curtly: "And you will be his slaves"—a bitter reminder of where Israel came from. "And in that day you will cry out because of your king, whom you have chosen for yourselves; but God will not answer you" (8:18).

This lesson reflects the running debate within the biblical tradition about the relative merits of kingship as a compromise of God's sovereignty (reiterated in Deut. 17:8-20). This suspicion of centralized authority continues into the book of Chronicles, which, as Jacques Ellul has shown, consistently evaluates kings who were militarily, economically, and politically strong as "evil in the sight of the Lord," and conversely portrays weak kings as good (1991:46ff.). "For every king there was a prophet," he adds, who "was most often a severe critic of royal acts." Ellul claims we can find no other historiographic tradition, ancient or modern, that is as critical of its own state as is the Hebrew Bible.

Other Lessons: The *BCP* lesson is Gen. 3:1-21, abbreviated by the *LBW* and Catholic lessons. If 1 Samuel 8 narrates the "fall of politics," this reading offers the primal account of the "politics of the Fall." Here is the archetypal story of human alienation from God, from the creation and from each other which drives them from the "garden." At the center of the text is the triangle of deception:

- Serpent "seduces" Woman to doubt God (vv. 1-5);
- Woman "seduces" Man to eat from the tree "in the middle of the garden" (vv. 6f.);
- Man avoids God *and* responsibility (vv. 8-12).

The triangle is then reversed in the "consequential curse": there will be enmity between Serpent and Woman (vv. 14f.), between Woman and Man (v. 16), and between Man and garden (vv. 17-19).

SECOND LESSON: 2 CORINTHIANS 4:13—5:1

Paul continues his apostolic defense with an endorsement of the kind of faith reflected in Psalm 116 (2 Cor. 4:13 = Ps. 116:10). This psalm extols God's love in spite of "the snares of death" and "distress and anguish" (116:3), which echoes Paul's own argument in last Sunday's lesson. He follows this by apparently citing an early Christian credal formula concerning eschatological resurrection (v. 14; see Rom. 8:11; 1 Cor. 6:14; 1 Thess. 4:13-18). Paul's ability to endure suffering was rooted in a conviction about the ultimacy of resurrection. He closes this part of his argument with a benediction reiterating that the purpose of apostolic travail is not heroism but to "extend grace to more and more people," a nice image for the spread of God's Jubilee (v. 15).

   With a repeat of the opening refrain ("therefore, we do not lose heart," v. 16a; see 4:1), Paul turns again to dualistic language to describe his commitment to "things that are unseen" (v. 18). Whereas in the Romans lesson for Trinity Sunday it was "flesh vs. spirit" (8:12ff.), here it is a series of contrasts:

- outer nature wasting away vs. inner nature being renewed (v. 16);
- momentary affliction vs. eternal weight of glory beyond all comparison (v. 17);
- things seen are transient vs. things unseen are eternal (v. 18);
- earthly tent being destroyed vs. eternal heavenly house not made with hands (5:1);
- naked in mortality vs. clothed in life (5:4).

Again, these oppositions reflect an apocalyptic discourse, positing "two ages" that compete for human allegiance. Paul's is not the pietistic argument that if we "bear the cross" now we will be rewarded later with a "crown" in heaven. His argument is that the "unseen" (v. 18; see Rom. 8:24) is a kind of parallel reality that eclipses all present loyalties, all political arrangements of privilege and power, and all circumstances of suffering. The "earthly tent" is, like the "earthen vessels" of 4:7, a metaphor for the fraility of human existence (5:1). But Paul looks to "a building from God, a house not made with hands" (see Mark 14:58; Acts 17:24; Heb. 9:11), an apocalyptic symbol of God's true sovereignty, as in the "New Jerusalem" of Revelation 21.

GOSPEL: MARK 3:20-35

The lesson jumps over several key episodes that follow last Sunday's conflict at the synagogue. Jesus withdraws to the sea (3:7), where Mark "regenerates" the momentum of the narrative in a summary passage. He reiterates each characteristic element of Jesus' mission: discipleship ("a multitude followed," v. 7); healing of the "crowds" (vv. 9f.); and exorcism (v. 11f.). Jesus next ascends a mountain in Mosaic fashion (v. 13), but unlike the old Sinai story in which the people were not allowed to follow Moses (Exod. 19:16-25), Jesus summons his leadership group to meet with him there. There is more to this story than just the commissioning of the disciples to take up the mission of liberation, however (vv. 14f.). Jesus' action echoes Joshua's appointment of leaders on the eve of Israel's dramatic crossing into the promised land (see Joshua 3–4). And his "naming of the Twelve" is an unmistakable allusion to the twelve tribes (see Genesis 49; Numbers 1). Christians have wrongly interpreted this symbol in terms of supercessionist theology, as if the apostolic church somehow was *replacing* Israel. Quite the contrary; Jesus' action here intends a *renewal* of the original Israelite tribal confederacy. This correlates with

Jesus' inaugural proclamation: the "kingship of God" is restored, here and now (Mark 1:15).

Today's lesson picks up the story after this dramatic political move, as Jesus returns home, where he is again engulfed by the importunate crowd (vv. 19f.). In the ensuing episode the stakes are raised for Jesus' "retribalization movement." His own family believes he has gone too far, and, "convinced he is out of his mind" (v. 21), urges him to cease and desist. To make matters worse, scribes from Jerusalem are launching an ideological counteroffensive (v. 22). The composition of 3:20-35 is a "sandwich," a favorite Markan technique of beginning one story, interrupting it with another, and then returning to the original story. This narrative structure establishes a relationship between the two episodes:

A	3:20f.	Jesus' family comes to "get" him
B	3:22-30	scribes from Jerusalem come to "get" him;
		he defines his mission over against them
A´	3:31-34	Jesus' family summons him;
		he defines his mission over against them.

Let us take the "outer" part of the sandwich first.

In Mediterranean antiquity the kinship system rigidly determined personality and identity, controlled vocational prospects, and facilitated overall socialization. The text of v. 21 is clear that Jesus' family sought to reign him in, not only for his protection but for the sake of their own reputation. In v. 31, perhaps further motivated by Jesus' clash with the scribal investigators, family members continue their efforts to restrain him. Jesus understands that in order to weave an alternative social fabric the most basic conventions and constraints of kinship must be questioned: "Who are my mother and my brothers?" (v. 33). Mark uses spatial tension to intensify this break: contrary to what we would expect, the disciples and the crowd are "inside" the home, while the family is "outside." Jesus concludes the scene by redefining kinship as "whoever does the will of God" (v. 35). In Jesus' retribalization movement, even the most basic social unit must be reordered under God's sovereignty.

Sandwiched inside this kinship conflict is the eruption of patently ideological warfare between Jesus and officials from the capital. Notice how tightly knit the two accusations are:

family	3:21	"He is beside himself"
scribes	3:22	"He is possessed"

Both the private sphere of the clan and the public sphere of the state equate the prevailing order with personal sanity and political sanctity. Smarting from Jesus' repudiation of their authority (see 2:6ff.), the scribes attempt to undermine Jesus' popular standing by charging that he is in the service of the "prince of demons." Jesus' deviant practice of exorcism, which liberates people *from* scribal domination (see 1:21-28) and *for* Jubilee economics and retribalized politics, must be dismissed as demonic. Who is "sane" in this polarized atmosphere obviously depends upon whose point of view we adopt.

Jesus masterfully turns his accusers' words back upon them, a strategy he will employ later with other Jerusalem leaders (see 11:27ff.). He poses a riddle that suggests the inevitability of insurrection in a corrupt and contradictory social order (vv. 24-26):

> How can Satan cast out Satan?
>   A divided kingdom cannot stand;
>   A divided house cannot stand;
> Satan divided (in revolt against himself)
> cannot stand but is coming to an end.

Kingdom (see 6:23; 11:10; 13:8) and *house* (see 11:17; 13:34f.) are key political metaphors in Mark's narrative, symbolizing the state and its symbolic center, the Temple. Jesus is thus returning the scribal repudiation by aligning their doomed Temple-state with Satan. He then makes his intentions clear, likening his mission to a thief who "must bind the strong man in order to ransack the goods in his house" (v. 27).

Mark has chosen this acrimonious debate to introduce Jesus' discourse of parables (v. 23). Parables in the Hebrew Bible are allegorical stories with thinly veiled political meanings (see Numbers 24; Ezekiel 17), such as the prophet Nathan's parable to David that unmasked his murderous abuse of power (see 2 Sam. 12:1-15). The Parable of the Strong Man will emerge as one of Mark's master metaphors. Later in the story Jesus will "break into" the Jerusalem Temple, "cast out" the true "thieves," and put a ban on the "goods" of that "house" (11:15-17). He will then insist it "cannot stand" (13:2) and exhorts his disciples to "keep watch" as the "house" awaits its true Lord (13:34f.).

The answer to the riddle of whether Satan can cast out Satan, then, is that Jesus (a.k.a. the "stronger one" heralded by John the Baptist back in 1:7), intends to overthrow the reign of the "strong man" (a.k.a. the scribal establishment represented by the demon back in 1:24). Mark appears to have taken his cue from Isaiah: "The captives of the strong one will be liberated; the prey of the tyrant will be rescued" (Isa. 49:24f.). This parable reveals the concrete political geography of Jesus' apocalyptic struggle with Satan initiated in 1:13, a battle not only for the people but for history itself.

Jesus ends the debate by issuing a blanket pardon, dealing a final blow to the debt code (v. 28), the first of several solemn "Amen" sayings in Mark. Excluded by definition, however, are those who demonize acts of healing and justice (vv. 29f.). As Juan Luis Segundo puts it, "The real sin against the Holy Spirit is refusing to recognize, with 'theological' joy, some concrete liberation that is taking place before one's very eyes."

HOMILETICAL REFLECTIONS

The lessons this Sunday could not be more political, nor more relevant to the struggle of Christians to be faithful in the context of the American empire. 1 Samuel warns that a people freed from Egyptian slavery will, if and when they choose a centralized monarchy, only set about recreating Pharaoh's society of domination (1 Sam. 8:8, 17). Yet Israel chooses to "be like the other nations" (8:20) despite the stern warning of Deut. 17:16: "You must never return that way again." It proves the truth of the old African American proverb: "It is easier to get the people out of Egypt than to get Egypt out of the people."

The Gospel lesson dramatizes the widening rift between Jesus, who wishes to renew the vision of a decentralized, covenant community, and the two pillars of the sociopolitical status quo—the clan and the state. The strategies of both threatened entities are predictable. Jesus' family tries to pull him out of circulation, no doubt "for his own good," while the political leaders would neutralize him by identifying him with the mythic national arch-demon. In modern America this would be tantamount to calling Jesus a "terrorist" or "Communist." Jesus responds by going on the offensive, interrogating the legitimacy of the public authorities. However unsettling the Strong Man Parable's metaphor of criminal breaking-and-entering may seem to modern Christians, the advent of the Lord as a "thief in the night" was one of the most enduring early Christian traditions (see Matt. 24:43; 1 Thess. 5:2, 4; 2 Peter 3:10; Rev. 3:3; 16:15). Jesus' commitment to the sovereignty of God made him unafraid to pick a fight with those claiming "leadership." Does ours?

Paul followed in Jesus' footsteps more than he is given credit for. His invocation of the "unseen" reality and the "heavenly building" (2 Cor. 4:18f.) undermined all public claims to greatness or power. It was his appeal to God's alternative authority that landed him in jail so often. This apparently was as embarrassing to the Corinthians of old as it is to our

North American churches. Furnish notes that the phrase "life of Jesus" in 2
Cor. 4:11 may have been

> a slogan among Paul's opponents in Corinth, and that it referred to Jesus'
> sensational powers which they sought to imitate in their own ministry.
> Against this, Paul would be contending that God's power is disclosed in
> weakness and suffering. (1984:283)

Today's lessons should give us pause to consider how politically domesticated our churches are, and how that prohibits us from risking our "earthly
tents" so that "grace might extend to more and more people."

Fourth Sunday after Pentecost
Eleventh Sunday in OrdinaryTime
Proper 6

Lectionary	First Lesson	Psalm	Second Lesson	Gospel
Revised Common	1 Sam. 15:34–16:13 or Ezek. 17:22-24	Psalm 20 or Ps. 92:1-4, 12-15	2 Cor. 5:6-10 (11-13), 14-17	Mark 4:26-34
Episcopal (BCP)	Ezek. 31:1-6, 10-14	Psalm 92 or Ps. 92:1-4, 12-15	2 Cor. 5:1-10	Mark 4:26-34
Roman Catholic	Ezek. 17:22-24	Ps. 92:2-3, 13-16	2 Cor. 5:6-10	Mark 4:26-34
Lutheran (LBW)	Ezek. 17:22-24	Ps. 92:1-5,(6-10), 11-14	2 Cor. 5:1-10	Mark 4:26-34

FIRST LESSON: I SAMUEL 15:34—16:13

This Sunday offers another story of the "passing of the mantle." Two weeks ago we saw the eclipse of Eli by Samuel, and today's reading is about David's eclipse of Saul, the first king of Israel. No sooner have Israel's tribal leaders rejected Samuel's warnings about kingship (8:19-22) than the story of Saul commences (9:1ff.). His recognition by God echoes the call of Moses: "He shall save my people from the hand of the Philistines, for I have seen the suffering of my people, and their cry has come to me" (9:16; see Exod. 3:7-10). Saul's anointing by Samuel, the accompanying prophetic signs (including a lottery), and his prowess at war all confirm Saul's status as king (chaps. 10–11).

But Samuel continues to insist that this is a compromise on God's part resulting from Israel's lack of faith in the ability of God to protect them (10:17-19; 12:1-13). And as he instructs the people "in the rights and duties of kingship" (10:25) he warns them that the rules of covenant have not changed (12:14-25). The narrative also notes that many of the tribal military leaders refused to go along with the new arrangement (10:27; 11:12). Almost immediately Saul tries to expropriate the cultic authority of Samuel, and this begins his decline (13:8-14). But his fatal error is taking booty from the Canaanite wars, against the express command of God (15:1-9). So, just as Samuel's prophetic career began by having to speak harsh words to Eli about God's judgment (3:2-18), so does it end having to tell Saul that "the LORD has rejected you from being king over Israel" (15:10-29).

The narrative of David's anointing has three parts, each consisting of God's command to Samuel and his response:

- a reluctant Samuel is dispatched to locate the new king (16:1-5)
- Jesse's sons are considered (vv. 6-11);
- David is chosen and anointed (vv. 12-13).

There are two points to this story. First, as Samuel had feared (15:2), royal succession will be nasty business (vv. 14ff.), confirming last week's warnings about the nature of power! Second, God's choices for political leadership do not conform to conventional expectations. Instead of the charismatic Eliab, the "obvious" choice to Samuel, God picks someone from "offstage" whom none of the principals even considered. God continues to work subversively, even in the context of the Israelite monarchy.

Other Lessons: Ezekiel 17:22-24 (Catholic and *LBW*) and 31:1-14 (*BCP*) are both tree parables that protest against imperial politics (see below, Gospel). In the first parable the prophet attempts to persuade Israel's rulers to remain faithful to God even though they dwell in the shadow of the "tall cedars" of the surrounding empires, and to resist the temptation to forge security through military alliances (17:1-21). God promises to raise up Israel "that it may produce branches and bear fruit, and become a noble cedar . . . in the shade of its branches will nest winged creatures of every kind" (v. 23), an image that Mark's Jesus will cite (Mark 4:32). This is so that "all the trees of the field shall know that I bring low the high tree, I make high the low tree" (Ezek. 17:24).

The second tree parable satirizes imperial Egypt. The prophet asks Pharaoh: "Who are you like in your greatness?" (31:2), but them reminds Pharaoh about Assyria, which also "towered high above all the trees of the field; its boughs grew large and its branches long. . . . All the birds of the air made their nests in its boughs" (vv. 5-6). Assyria was brought down, and Ezekiel parodies: "On its fallen trunk settle all the birds of the air" (v. 13). This parable may be alluding to the legend of the Tower of Babel: "All this in order that no trees by the waters may grow to lofty height or set their tops among the clouds" (v. 14; see Gen. 11:4 [above, Homiletical Reflections on Pentecost Sunday]).

SECOND LESSON: 2 CORINTHIANS 5:1-17

The epistle (of varying lengths among the lectionaries) takes up Paul's closing argument in his defense of his apostolic credentials. The first part of the passage revisits the notion of the frailty of life in the body (vv. 2-10). The "groaning" and "sighs" (vv. 2, 4) echo Paul's eloquent contention in

Romans that the whole creation is waiting for the children of God to bring liberation, while "we ourselves . . . groan inwardly . . . waiting for adoption as children, the redemption of our bodies" (Rom. 8:19-23).

The image of "putting on" new clothes over nakedness (v. 3) is baptismal language that Paul often uses in parenetic exhortation (see Rom. 13:12-14; Gal. 3:27; Col. 3:10-14). Baptism symbolizes the "Spirit's guarantee" of total transformation—being "swallowed up in life" (vv. 4f.; see 1 Cor. 15:53f., "death is swallowed up in victory"). This eschatological assertion clarifies the otherwise confusing discussion of being "at home" in the body that follows (vv. 6-10). Paul's language should not be interpreted in terms of the Hellenistic contempt for the body, which equated salvation with release from the "prison" of the flesh into an ethereal state. This whole discussion is predicated instead upon the apocalyptic assumption of the resurrection of the body (vv. 4, 10).

To conclude his argument Paul once again alludes to his apostolic opponents (vv. 11-13). Apparently they alleged that he had failed to demonstrate the "outward" manifestations of apostolic status: the ecstatic spiritual experiences and homiletic eloquence so highly valued in Hellenistic religion and philosophy (v. 12). Elsewhere Paul denounces the art of rhetorical "persuasion" as mere sophistry (1 Cor. 2:4; Gal. 1:10). Here, however, he claims that he does "persuade," but with a clean conscience before the One who reads the heart (v. 11). But this may be a parody on the Corinthians' seduction by status-seekers: "We are not commending ourselves but giving you reason to be *proud* of us so that you may be able to answer those who *pride* themselves on position . . ." (v. 12). If Paul is ever "beside himself" in spiritual ecstasy it is a private matter between him and God (see 12:2-5; below, the Seventh Sunday after Pentecost). Apostolic character should rather be judged by "right minded" commitment to the church at Corinth (v. 13). The principle of subordinating spiritual experience to communal service is articulated by Paul at length in 1 Corinthians 14.

In an oblique reference to the cost of apostolic witness, Paul now employs two juridicial metaphors to describe his group's commitment to the kind of love that gives up its own life for the other. The love of Christ "holds them in custody" because they "have come to the judgment" that he died for everyone (v. 14). "Therefore all have died" is another assertion that the old order of death is passing away, freeing them to live for others (v. 15). That this is a reference to the apocalyptic "new age" is confirmed by the statement that they no longer view things from "a human point of view," and that in Christ we are "new creations—behold the old has passed away" (vv. 16f.). Paul's ability to existentialize the radical transformative dualism of apocalyptic was part of his genius.

GOSPEL: MARK 4:26-34

After breaking with family and state (see last week's lesson), Jesus again retires to the sea, this time to reflect on the state of the messianic mission. Here Mark reports the first of two extended sermons. This sermon begins when Jesus gets into a boat (4:1), and ends when he embarks to "the other side" (vv. 35f.). In a series of seed parables Jesus speaks frankly of the obstacles to the discipleship adventure and enjoins patient hope using images drawn from the hardship and wisdom of daily peasant life.

Parables have typically been preached in North American churches as "earthly stories with heavenly meanings." This, however, is exactly what they are *not*. Rather, Mark's Jesus illustrates the sovereignty of God in the most concrete possible terms, using images even illiterate peasants could understand. Jesus no doubt struggled to explain his vision for personal and collective life because it was so much at odds with the prevailing order, and thus with the experience of his audience. Parables offer recognizable scenarios, drawing the audience in, but then throw surprise twists in order to challenge its assumptions about what is possible.

In order to articulate what he stands *for*, Jesus begins with what the people stand *on*—the land itself. The first half of the sermon is organized around the famous parable of the sower (vv. 3-8) and its explanation (vv. 14-22), bracketed by a thematic refrain exhorting the audience to "Listen!" (vv. 3, 9, 23). In the middle of the sower story Jesus defines parables as a discourse directed toward those in denial, alluding to the call of Isaiah (vv. 10-13; see above, Trinity Sunday). The second half of the sermon begins with some warnings about not succumbing to the "realism" of those who benefit from the status quo—"Beware what you hear!" (vv. 21-25). We then come to two more seed parables—one about means and one about ends—which constitute this week's Gospel (vv. 26-32).

Against the cynical economic "determinism" of the dominant social order ("to the one who has more will be given. . . ," v. 25) Jesus pits the patient hope of the farmer:

> And he said: The sovereignty of God is as if someone should scatter seed upon the ground . . . (v. 26)
> And he said: With what can we compare the sovereignty of God? . . . It is like a grain of mustard seed which, when sown upon the ground . . . (v. 30)

Mark's audience doubtless wondered when and how the miraculous harvest promised in the sower parable would be realized (v. 8). The answer is that the sower "knows not how" the growth occurs (v. 27), that "the earth bears fruit of itself" (v. 28, a reference back to the yield of v. 20). This is not advocating passivity but reasserting the divine economy of grace. Sabbath wisdom recognizes that humans must not seek to control the land but rather to live within its limits.

But this parable is given urgency in v. 29 by an allusion to Joel 3:13: "Put in the sickle, for the harvest is ripe." In the apocalyptic tradition of holy war, Joel's prophetic oracle foresees God gathering the nations that have oppressed Israel for judgment (Joel 3:9-16). Mark's point is to assure the listener that God will vindicate those who work faithfully, despite the appearances of history. Mark will have more to say about such "revolutionary patience" in Jesus' second sermon and its two apocalyptic parables (13:28ff.).

Jesus' sermon concludes with an insistence that despite long odds, the smallest seed can indeed take root in a hostile world and flourish (4:30-32). Here the focus is again upon the miraculous harvest, symbolized now as "the greatest of all shrubs in whose large branches all the birds of the air can make nests" (v. 32). This is a common metaphor for political sovereignty in the Hebrew Bible, and thus places Jesus' entire sermon firmly in an anti-imperial context. Perhaps the earliest tradition of tree parables is found in Judges, where Jotham criticizes Abimelech's murderous grab for power (Judg. 9:1-21). In that parable the olive, fig, and vine all refuse to abandon their productive tasks to become "king." The bramble, however, says: "If in good faith you are anointing me king over you, then come and take refuge in my shade; but if not let fire come out of the bramble and devour the cedars of Lebanon" (9:15).

We have briefly considered the tree parables of Ezekiel above. Daniel, a manifesto of resistance to Hellenistic imperialism, also uses this image. King Nebuchadnezzar dreams of "a tree at the center of the earth . . . its top reached to heaven . . . and the birds of the air nested in its branches, and from it all living beings were fed" (Dan. 4:11f.). Once again the prophet promises that the hubris of empire will be judged, and in order to avoid having the tree "cut down" (4:14), Daniel exhorts the king to "atone for your sins with justice and for your iniquities with mercy to the oppressed" (4:27). It is in the tradition of such parables that Mark's Jesus "speaks the Word," carefully interpreting their political allusions to the disciples (Mark 4:33f.).

HOMILETICAL REFLECTIONS

This week's lessons provide an opportunity to preach about the biblical call to personal and political transformation. The story of God's choice of David over Jesse's sons establishes the fact that leadership qualities cannot be judged by appearances. This is precisely what Paul is trying to persuade the Corinthians of, so they "may be able to answer those who pride themselves on a person's position" (2 Cor. 5:12). It is also the point of Jesus' seed parables.

In Mark's time the tiny client-state of Judea was, to use Ezekiel's image, just another "tree of the field" being sustained "by the streams flowing" from Rome (Ezek. 31:4). And within Palestine Mark's community was a small, persecuted minority. What chance did followers of Jesus have? Yet the parable of the mustard seed proposes exactly such a mismatch! Mark repudiates the imperial myth of omnipotence, exhorting disciples to "keep their eyes on the prize" of a Jubilee that will enfranchise everyone—no matter how remote that possibility might seem. Yet at the same time the parable of the patient farmer reminds one of Gandhi's counsel to focus on the work at hand and to "leave the results of our work to God."

Jesus the parable-spinner in Mark is no guru dispensing arcane secrets or pious platitudes. He is a popular educator using language that peasants can understand, images they can relate to from their experience, and stories that portray *them* as subjects of the sovereignty of God. In so doing he sows both hope and patience among them, insisting that the tall trees can be brought down and that the smallest of seeds will bear Jubilary fruit.

Fifth Sunday after Pentecost
Twelfth Sunday in Ordinary Time
Proper 7

Lectionary	First Lesson	Psalm	Second Lesson	Gospel
Revised Common	I Sam. 17: (1a, 4-11, 19-23), 32-49 or I Sam. 17:57—18:5, 10-16 or Job 38:1-11	Ps. 9:9-20 or Psalm 133 or Ps. 107:1-3, 23-32	2 Cor. 6:1-13	Mark 4:35-41
Episcopal (BCP)	Job 38:1-11, 16-18	Ps. 107:1-32 or 107:1-3, 23-32	2 Cor. 5:14-21	Mark 4:35-41; (5:1-20)
Roman Catholic	Job 38:1, 8-11	Ps. 107:1, 23-31	2 Cor. 5:14-17	Mark 4:35-41
Lutheran (LBW)	Job 38:1-11	Ps. 107:1-3, 23-32	2 Cor. 5:14-21	Mark 4:35-41

FIRST LESSON: I SAMUEL 17

The lesson begins with a terrible refrain that typified the struggle of the Hebrews in their promised land: "Now the Philistines gathered their armies for battle" (17:1). Norman Gottwald notes that the Philistines were probably installed in Canaan as vassals by the Egyptians in order to buttress the latter's imperial control over the region:

> By 1050 B.C.E. [they] were posing a serious threat to the mountainous heartland of Israel. The Philistines had the advantage of oligarchic leadership, unlike the divisive Canaanite city-states, and their iron weaponry and mobile strike force made them effective fighters in the hill country. (1985:319)

The biblical narratives clearly identify the Philistines as the most stubborn military and political threat to the Israelite tribal confederacy.

According to 1 Samuel, the Philistines' decisive defeat of Eli's tribal coalition and capture of the ark was one of the primary factors that led to the clamour for kingship in Israel (4:4-22). The balance of power then shifted back and forth: "There was hard fighting against the Philistines all the days of Saul" (14:52). Apparently the aim of the Philistine lords was to force Israel to become their agricultural producers under a tributary relationship. Gottwald believes that Israel's integration into the imperial-feudal grid system of Philistia would have spelled doom for her own autonomous institutions—a virtual return to bondage in Egypt. This may be reflected in the account of the ark's captivity in Ashdod, which echoes God's judgments on Pharaoh (5:6ff; 6:6).

Interestingly, the biblical depictions of these archrivals are full of satire. After their capture of the ark the Philistine cult is parodied, as the

42

image of the god Dagon keeps falling over while the people are inflicted with tumors (5:1-12). In the end the Philistines must make a guilt offering of five "golden tumors and five gold mice"—probably symbolizing the hegemony of the five Philistine city-states (6:1-5)—while the ark returns "on its own" to Israel (chaps. 5–6). Another parody is found in the story of David and Goliath, this week's lesson. This story obviously has been inserted here, since it contradicts the narrative's flow (David is unknown to Saul in this episode; for example, 17:58). Moreover, the description of the "champion" soldier Goliath, with its exaggerations of his physical size and elaborate defensive armament and offensive weaponry, makes the reader wonder whether he might not be a symbol for Philistine military might itself (17:4-11).

David comes on the scene (after the digression of 17:12-18, omitted by the lesson) in time the hear the offer of a reward for Goliath's demise (vv. 25f., also omitted). This latter element, so characteristic of a folktale, functions to underline David's piety: his concern is not the reward but Goliath's "defiance of the living God" (vv. 26, 36). The parody develops through a series of contrasts:

- David is "just a boy," Goliath a "warrior from his youth" (v. 33);
- David cannot walk in his armor, Goliath towers in his (vv. 5f., 38f.);
- David goes to battle with the tools of a shepherd, Goliath with those of a professional mercenary (vv. 40-46).

The punchline comes as David returns his opponent's taunts: "You come to me with a sword and spear and javelin; but I come to you in the name of the LORD . . . so that all the earth may know that there is a God in Israel, and that all this assembly may know that the LORD does not save by sword and spear" (vv. 45-47). This is a *didactic* story, confirmed by the fact that the report of the battle itself is brief and almost matter-of-fact (vv. 48f.). The moral of the tale is that "there was no sword in David's hand" (v. 50)—the parody is not just of the Philistines, but of *trust in militarism*!

Other Lessons: The *LBW* lesson (Job 38:1-11) is the beginning of God's answer to Job "out of the whirlwind" (abbreviated by the Catholic and slightly expanded by the *BCP* lesson). These are God's first words in edgewise since the opening "heavenly court" scenes of 1:6-12 and 2:1-6. They come on the heels of long discourses by Job and his "comforters": Eliphaz (chaps. 4f., 15, and 22), Bildad (chaps. 8, 18, and 25), Zophar (chaps. 11 and 20), and Elihu (chaps. 32–37). God's "defense" is, of course, simply an account of the majesty of creation. This text connects with the Gospel lesson in its reflections upon the might of the sea (vv. 8-

11; 16-18). The creation metaphors of this discourse still endure—as does the argument itself!

SECOND LESSON: 2 CORINTHIANS 5:18—6:13

This lesson completes the apostle's self-characterization that we have been reading for the last three weeks. I will pick it up where the RCL left off last week (5:17); those using the other three lectionaries may wish to consult last week's notes. Paul has just declared the "apocalypse now" through the new creation in Christ (5:17). But so that no one misunderstands this as a declaration of war on God's enemies, Paul immediately characterizes God's purpose as one of reconciliation (vv. 18f.). Furnish contends Paul is citing a traditional theological forumula here, and notes that it consists of three essential assertions (1984:334ff.).

The first assertion, stated not once but twice, is the extraordinary notion of "God reconciling the world to Godself" (v. 19). This undermines the idea of Christ's death as "substitutionary atonement" for an angry God. God is the *initiator*, not the *recipient*, of this reconciliation. The second key assertion is that this was a Self-sacrifice accomplished "in Christ." If God is the *who* and Christ the *how*, then the third assertion is *what* reconciliation means. It is nothing less than God's unilateral declaration of Jubilee by "not counting their trespasses against them" (v. 19; see the Preface). In Paul's theology, the divine economy of grace is the antithesis of the debt system: "The free gift is not like the trespass" (Rom. 5:15).

This Jubilee empowers Paul's "ministry of reconciliation" (v. 18; Gk. *katallagees*). Frances Young and David Ford (1987:175) have shown that this term originally referred to an exchange of money in repayment of a debt (we still speak today of "reconciling a bank statement"). The apostle is an "ambassador" for Christ, a title used in the Greek-speaking Roman empire for the official envoys of Caesar. God's official "appeal" through such emissaries is: "Be reconciled to God" (v. 20). To participate in this new social order we must *accept* this divine reconciliation of accounts. Furnish notes that here "the indicative mood gives way to the imperative" (1984:348), a transition typical of Paul's hortatory style (see Rom. 12:1ff.). We are invited to do things not out of obligation but because they are divine *realities* waiting to be *realized* in our lives: God has reconciled with the world, therefore be reconciled with God!

To accept this new social order in which debt has been abolished is to participate in what Paul calls "the justice of God" (v. 21). This famous Pauline phrase, which appears some ten times in his letters, refers specifically to the fact that *God's* justice does not cohere with *our* sense of economic "fairness." After all, the unindebted One "took on debt for our sake," in order to liberate us from its totalitarianism (see also Rom. 8:3). But if we, like Paul, wish to "cooperate" with God, we must be prepared to practice this Jubilee ourselves; otherwise the divine economy of grace is "in vain" (6:1). Paul quotes Isa. 49:8, a hymn to the liberation of Israel from captivity, and then existentializes it: "Now is that day!" (v. 2). His rhetorical strategy is not unlike Luke's in Jesus' inaugural sermon: after reading Isaiah's vision of the Jubilee he announces to the synagogue that "Today this scripture has been fulfilled" (Luke 4:21).

I would paraphrase Paul's argument in 5:19—6:2 thus:

> In Christ God was declaring a Jubilee ("reconciling our accounts") by canceling all our outstanding debts, and now entrusts to us the job of making this declaration known. We are ambassadors (of this new "social state") for Christ, and through us God makes this appeal. We plead with you on behalf of Christ (the head of this new "social state") to accept God's reconciliation! For our sake God transferred the debt to him who was unindebted, so that in him we might live out the justice of God. In cooperation with him, then, we entreat you not to receive this Jubilee without effect (that is, without practicing it)! . . . Behold, now is the time to start!

This text shows that for Paul, Christ's "new order" has an irreducible social, political, and economic character.

Paul's final iteration of his apostolic credentials come in vv. 3-10. He pleads innocent to allegations that he has obstructed the practice of Jubilee (v. 3), anticipating his appeal to the Corinthians to join in economic sharing with other churches (see next week's lesson). Then, as he did in 4:5ff., he insists that true "servants of God" can only be commended by *suffering* and *integrity*, and offers two lists to prove he embodies both qualities. The list of sufferings is structured as three groups of three:

- the general lot of an apostle: affliction, hardship, and calamity (v. 4);
- his record of political persecution: beatings, imprisonments, and riots (v. 5a; all in the plural!);
- and the wear and tear of his self-supporting ministry: tiring labor, sleeplessness, and hunger (v. 5b).

At the top of the list of integrity is Paul's "great endurance" of the things named above (v. 4). The rest of the list sounds almost like a traditional "virtue list" found in parenetic tradition (vv. 6f.; see Gal. 5:22f.; Phil. 4:8; Col. 3:12-15; Eph. 4:1-3). The lists conclude with a favorite catechetical metaphor of Paul, the "weapons of justice" (v. 7b; see 1 Thess. 5:8; Rom. 13:12; Eph. 6:13-17).

This represents Paul's self-description; what follows is how he is perceived by others (vv. 8-10). The seven antitheses again articulate Paul's apocalyptic faith. Though the world may see him as an *imposter*, or *obscure*, or *poor*, in the alternative reality of God he is *true*, *well-known*, and *enriching*. Paul's discourse closes with a final indicative/imperative appeal. Because his apostolic group reaches out to the Corinthians with "widened hearts," they should reciprocate: "Widen your hearts also!" (vv. 11-13).

GOSPEL: MARK 4:35-41

The second major section of Mark's Gospel opens and closes with a boat trip (4:35-41; 8:13-21). These sea journeys signal a new kind of symbolic action that will dramatize the concrete social and economic shape of the sovereignty of God. Scholars have puzzled over the fact that in this section Mark, otherwise the sparest of the Gospel writers, is curiously redundant. He narrates two perilous crossings of the Sea of Galilee during storms (here and 6:45-53) and two feedings of hungry masses in the wilderness (6:33-44; 8:1-9). Jesus' healings, too, are neatly organized into pairs: two Jews (5:21-43) and two Gentiles (7:24-37). And the exorcism of the Gerasene demoniac (5:1-20) has clear similarities with Jesus' inaugural exorcism back in the Capernaum synagogue (1:21ff.).

We should remember that in storytelling there is an essential relationship between *form* and *content*. We can better observe Mark's narrative strategy in this section if we step away from the chronological flow of events in order to identify a pattern. We find two roughly parallel "cycles" of ministry in the first half of the Gospel:

	"JEWISH" SIDE *1st cycle*	"GENTILE" SIDE *2nd cycle*
Inaugural exorcisms	1:21-28	5:1-20
Paired healings	5:22-43	7:24-37
Feeding of multitudes	6:32-44	8:1-10
Incomprehension of loaves	6:51f.	8:14-21

Each cycle takes place on different sides of the sea, which Jesus and his disciples are traversing back and forth by boat. The function of this pattern is to emphasize that Jesus' mission of proclamation, exorcism, and healing took place in both spheres of Mark's world: the Jewish and the non-Jewish.

The Sea of Galilee lies at the geographic heart of Galilee. In 4:35 Jesus and his disciples embark on the first of several journeys to "the other side," an area equated in Mark's narrative with everything east of the Jordan river. From Mark's Jewish point of view, this was Gentile territory, firmly under the control of Rome. Thus it represents the alien and threatening world of social, cultural, and political foreigners. (It is important to understand that Mark is speaking symbolically here, since Jewish and non-Jewish populations were not in fact strictly segregated on opposite sides of the sea.) Despite the "otherness" of non-Jews, Mark's Jesus is determined to bring the gospel of liberation to their "side." This project is articulated in four journeys in Mark 4–8. There are three boat voyages to the other side of the sea, though only two are successful (5:1 and 8:22; the crossing of 6:45 is unsuccessful). In the midst of these voyages there is a long, circuitous trip by land to the northwest coastal cities of Tyre and Sidon, a region also considered "out" of the Jewish sphere (7:24, 31).

Upon conclusion of his parables sermon Jesus invites his disciples to embark on the first of these boat trips (4:35). During the crossing a storm blows up, and the little boat begins to take on water (v. 37). The disciples, among whom were fishermen experienced on the sea, realize they are going down. In a moment of high pathos, they scream at their dozing leader: "Master, do you not care if we perish?!" (v. 38). Jesus rebukes the storm (v. 39), but unlike Ps. 107:23-30 to which it alludes, this episode ends not with relief or triumph but with Jesus and the disciples wondering about each other:

> Jesus: "Do you not yet have faith?" (v. 40).
> Disciples: "Who then is this that even the sea and wind obey
>   him?" (v. 41).

Note the similarity between the disciples' reaction and the crowd's incredulity following Jesus' inaugural exorcism: "*What is this? . . .* He commands even the unclean spirits and they *obey him!*" (1:27). Indeed, Jesus "silences" the storm here just as he did the demon there, suggesting some connection between the two stories.

Mark tells us that the disciples are more unnerved *after* Jesus silences the storm than they were in the midst of it (literally they "feared a great fear," 4:41)! Is this due to their awe before a nature miracle, or might it have more to do with their dread of actually having to complete this trip to the "other side"? We can answer this by seeing how this boat story (and its counterpart in 6:45-52) draws on archetypal symbols. Mark consistently refers to the freshwater lake as a "sea" in order to invoke images from the most primal narratives in the Hebrew tradition: the ark of Noah (Genesis 7–8); the crossing of the Red Sea (Exodus 14); and the Psalmic odes to storms (e.g., Ps. 48:7; 104:6-9, 24f.). But above all Mark draws on the tale of Jonah, the prophet commissioned to preach repentance to the imperial city-state of Ninevah (Jon. 1:1f.). Jonah fled from his task because he was unconcerned with the fate of non-Israelites under Ninevite oppression (4:11). So Jonah, like the disciples here, was caught up in a "great storm" (1:3f.). At first he slept through it, as does Jesus here (1:5f. = Mark 4:38), but was then thrown overboard to his infamous rendezvous with the "belly of the beast" (1:15-17). Ultimately Jonah learns his lesson and accomplishes his mission to the "great city" (3:1-10).

The wind and waves in Mark's harrowing sea stories symbolize everything that impedes Jesus' mission of boundary crossing. These cosmic forces of opposition suggest that the messianic task of social reconciliation was not only difficult but well-nigh inconceivable. Indeed, the enmity between Jew and Gentile was seen by most of Mark's contemporaries as the prototype of all human hostility, and the ideological and institutional structures of separation between them considered part of the natural order. No wonder then that in Mark's second crossing episode Jesus must *force* the disciples to get into the boat to go to the other side (6:45)! This explains Mark's characterization of Jesus' confrontation with the storm as an exorcism. The forces of resistance to his mission must be "silenced," and disciples must overcome their fear in order to follow in Jonah's footsteps preaching the good news that imperial oppression "will be overthrown" (Jon. 3:4). Indeed, the demise of the imperial "Legion" is the theme of the exorcism that follow, in Mark 5:1-20 (the alternate *BCP* lesson).

HOMILETICAL REFLECTIONS

The lessons invite us to reflect on the task of realizing God's invitation to reconciliation. We get a hint of this even in the battle legend of David and Goliath, for it presents a central conviction of the biblical "conquest" narratives. Unlike other historico-legendary traditions of military triumph and heroism in antiquity, whenever Israel prevailed in battle it is not portrayed as the result of *their* military proficiency. Israel defeats her opponents solely because "the LORD delivered the enemy into their hands." This is crucial for modern readers to understand about the "holy war" discourse of the Hebrew Bible. It represents a *repudiation* of the politics, economics, and technology of military security, not an ethical *justification* for them.

The first lesson begins: "The Philistines stood on the mountain on the one side, and Israel stood on the mountain on the other side, with a valley between them" (1 Sam. 17:3). There is a curious resonance here with the Gospel, which is about a stormy sea separating two "sides." In the latter case, however, the point is to cross over to the "other" to heal and liberate, not to defeat him in battle. The sea crossings in Mark symbolized the formidable project of peacemaking between the "two humanities" of Jew and Gentile. This was considered central to the first Christians' self-understanding, as exemplified by the eloquent exposition on reconciliation found in Ephesians 2 (see below, the Ninth Sunday after Pentecost). It is no accident, then, that a boat on the sea was one of the earliest symbols of the church—and remains today in the international ecumencial movement.

Paul also presents his mission as one of reconciliation—but is candid about the costs of such work. With such consistent testimony in the New Testament, we must ask why it is so difficult for the North American church to embrace the vocation of reconciliation today? Our world, balanced on the scales of gender, race, and class division and oppression, is in desperate need for "ambassadors" who are committed to embodying the "justice of God" (2 Cor. 5:20f.).

Sixth Sunday after Pentecost
Thirteenth Sunday in Ordinary Time
Proper 8

Lectionary	First Lesson	Psalm	Second Lesson	Gospel
Revised Common	2 Sam. 1:1, 17-27 or Wisd. 1:13-15; 2:23-24	Psalm 130 or 30 or Lam. 3:23-33	2 Cor. 8:7-15	Mark 5:21-43
Episcopal (BCP)	Deut. 15:7-11	Psalm 112	2 Cor. 8:1-9, 13-15	Mark 5:22-24, 35b-43
Roman Catholic	Wisd. 1:13-15, 2:23-24	Ps. 30:2, 4-6, 11-13	2 Cor. 8:7, 9, 13-15	Mark 5:21-24, 35b-43 or 5:21-43
Lutheran (LBW)	Lam. 3:22-33	Psalm 30	2 Cor. 8:1-9, 13-14	Mark 5:21-24a, 35-43 or 5:24b-34

FIRST LESSON: 2 SAMUEL 1:1, 17-27

We move into 2 Samuel with the report of Saul's death (1:1). His demise in battle against the Philistines is narrated in 1 Samuel 31, though this account differs from that of 2 Samuel 1:2-16. The lesson consists of David's funeral dirge for Saul, called in v. 18 "The Song of the Bow," which was recorded in the "Book of Jashar," a lost collection of ancient Hebrew hero-ballads (see Josh. 10:13; 1 Kings 8:12f.). Saul's death completes David's long-developing rise to power, and 2 Samuel 2 will narrate his return from expatriation and his anointing as king of Judah.

The story of Saul is certainly tragic; after all, the error that turned God against him was as much Samuel's fault as his own (see 1 Sam. 13:8-15). The narrator is really only interested in legitimating David's rise to power and so paints a very dark portrait of Saul's descent into jealous madness (beginning in 1 Samuel 18). Yet the ideology of the narrator is not so much anti-Saul as ambivalent about kingship. The fate of Saul illustrates the nature of power, for David too will err when he turns his hegemony toward personal ends (2 Sam. 11:1—12:3).

This ambivalence is reflected in the Song of the Bow. Traditional in its structure, it laments the loss of Saul and Jonathan (vv. 21, 24f.) and eulogizes their military exploits (vv. 22f.). But the real point of the the the dirge seems to be its threefold refrain:

> Alas! the Glory of Israel, Saul, slain upon your heights; How can the warriors have fallen?! (v. 19)

> How can the warriors have fallen—in the thick of the battle, slain upon your heights! (v. 25)

How can the warriors have fallen, the weapons of war have perished! (v. 27; NAB)

If the hero-legend of David and Goliath parodies those who trust in military strength, this song bemoans them. The biblical writers concede neither efficacy nor moral character to the nation's armed struggles.

Other Lessons: The lectionaries diverge sharply on this Sunday. The *LBW* lesson is taken from Lam. 3:22-33, which exhorts patience in the face of suffering in the conviction that God vindicates. Jesus' counsel in his Sermon on the Mount to "turn the other cheek" may come from this oracle (v. 30; see Matt. 5:39). The Catholic lesson is from the book of Wisdom, a first-century B.C.E. collection of sage sayings put in the mouth of King Solomon. The text is an interesting meditation on the fact that "God did not make death" (1:13; NAB), attributing its entry into the world to Satan (2:23f.).

The *BCP* lesson (Deut. 15:7-11) seems the most relevant to the other two lessons, which have to do with economic sharing and the poor. It concerns the sabbatical principle of the seventh year (15:1; see the Preface). The "remission of debt" is to be enacted within the Israelite community (though not with foreigners, v. 3) on the assurance that "there will be no one in need among you" (v. 4). The Deuteronomist is practical, exhorting Israelites to lend generously even though the seventh year of remission is close at hand (vv. 7-10), no doubt anticipating the human tendency to find self-serving exceptions to God's rules of generosity. The passage concludes with a remarkable statement:

> Since there will never cease to be some in need on the earth, I therefore command you, "Open you hand to the poor and needy neighbor in your land." (v. 11)

We Christians would do well to inscribe *that* on our hearts and learn to live by it!

SECOND LESSON: 2 CORINTHIANS 8:1-15

The epistle (abbreviated in various ways by each of the four lectionaries) is the first part of another lengthy Pauline appeal, this time concerning the sharing of wealth (chaps. 8–9). The occasion is a collection that Paul was orchestrating among his churches on behalf of poor Christians in Jerusalem (see 1 Cor. 16:1-4; Rom. 15:25-32; Gal. 2:10). Apparently the Corinthians had promised, but not yet delivered on, their participation in this project (vv. 10f.). Paul's initial exhortation is quite nuanced, however. He uses the example of other communities' generosity in order to cajole (vv. 1-5); directs but does not command the Corinthians (vv. 7f.); points to Christ's example (v. 9); gives strong "advice" (vv. 10f.); and explains the principle behind the practice (vv. 12-15). It is not that Paul is being tentative here; rather, he is concerned that the Corinthians will interpret his appeal according to expectations normal to the dominant culture around them.

The notion of one group or individual offering financial aid to another was certainly common in the Hellenistic world. However, such transactions were understood in terms of a "patron-client" relationship, described by Bruce Malina and Richard Rohrbaugh as

> socially fixed relations of generalized reciprocity between social unequals in which a lower-status person in need (called a client) has his needs met by having recourse for favors to a higher-status, well-situated person (called a patron). By being granted the favor, the client implicitly promises to pay back the patron whenever and however the patron determines. . . . The client relates to the patron as to a superior and more powerful kinsman, while the patron looks after his clients as he does his dependents. (1992:235)

The conventions of patronage functioned in economic, social, and political spheres. It was precisely the obligatory and unequal nature of this relationship that Paul wished to avoid.

From Paul's perspective the Corinthians are relatively well-off, at least compared with the church in Jerusalem and even in Macedonia (vv. 2, 7). But he is asking for their Christian solidarity, not their patronage (see 9:5-7). This is why here the project is not called a *collection*, as in 1 Cor. 16:1, but a "communal service" (Gk. *tēn koinōnian tēs diakonias*, 8:4), or a *generosity* (8:2; 9:11, 13), or even a *blessing* (9:5). Paul wants the Corinthians to understand this financial partnership in terms of God's economy of grace. Indeed the collection is called a "grace" (vv. 6, 19), but as Paul reminds them at the beginning and end of his appeal, it is one that merely reflects the grace of God (8:1; 9:14). Their largess can only faintly reflect God's "indescribable gift" (9:15).

Young and Ford have demonstrated that Paul uses economic metaphors throughout 2 Corinthians (1987:166ff.). The Spirit is a "downpayment" from God (1:22), for example, and the gospel a "treasure" (4:7). Twelve times in this epistle Paul describes his work as *diakonia* (the service appropriate to the slave class in the Hellenistic household). Later Paul uses the metaphor of passing on an inheritance: he will gladly be "spent" for the sake of his "children" (12:14f.). And in an earlier letter he compares his apostolic commission in terms of a "household economy" (1 Cor. 9:17; Gk. *oikonomian*).

Young and Ford believe that Paul's vocabulary of "abundance" throughout the correspondence (e.g., 1:5; 7:4; 9:14; 11:23) is intended to contrast the notion of "limited good" that characterized economic thought and discourse in antiquity.

> Subsistence with stability was the main aim of economic activity for most people, and the right to subsistence was closely bound to one's family and its inherited place in society. It was an economy in which equilibrium, not growth, was the ideal. This was supported by a network of relationships based on informal reciprocity, enforced by the powerful appeal to honour and shame. (1987:172)

Paul, they contend, understood God as the "central resource" who injects *unlimited* good into this economy. God's overflowing grace and gift should determine the circulation of goods and values in the church, not the economics of scarcity and patronage: "It is all for your sake, so that grace may extend to more and more people" (4:15). Young and Ford build a persuasive case—yet oddly never mention how the biblical concept of a divine economy of grace and gift is expressed most concretely in the Levitical vision of the Jubilee (see the Preface). I believe Paul understood the "Christ-event" as a "Jubilee-event" (see my comments last week on 5:19—6:2). *Grace*, traditionally understood by Protestants to lie at the heart of Paul's theology, pertains not just to "spiritual" matters, but invites us to Jubilee as a way of life.

Paul's lengthy discourse about apostleship and grace, then, has been laying the theological foundation for the real purpose of his letter: to persuade the Corinthians to embrace the Jubilee through economic solidarity with the "mother church" in Jerusalem. It is not irrelevant here that this latter church was, according to Luke's account in Acts, *already* practicing the redistributory economics of Jubilee (Acts 4:32-37; see my comments on Pentecost Sunday). Paul is urging his Hellenistic congregations to practice what the mother church had established as Christian "orthodoxy"—the economics of mutual aid (see Gal. 2:10). Furnish believes that Paul's assurance in v. 12 implies that the Corinthians may have been dragging their heels in contributing because they felt they could not give enough; they were, so to speak, "willing but not able." This would explain why Paul goes out of his way to praise the Macedonian churches, who "out of their extreme poverty . . . gave according to their means . . . and beyond" (8:2f.). Paul stresses that one can only give "what one has," the language alluding perhaps to Prov. 3:27f. (see 2 Cor. 9:6-12).

Paul now articulates the "golden rule" of Jubilee in a carefully crafted doublet:

> not that others should be relieved and you afflicted;
> rather, it is a matter of *equality*.
> But in this *kairos* your surplus should help their lack
> so that their surplus might help your lack
> in order that there may be *equality*. (vv. 13f.)

The term *equality*, so important to modernity, appears in the New Testament only here and in Col. 4:1 ("Masters, treat your slaves justly and as equals"—a phrase that effectively undermines the entire hierarchical structure of a slave-based society). This principle certainly echoes the spirit if not the exact vocabulary of Luke's description of the Pentecost church: "Great grace was among them all; there was not anyone in need among them, for as many as were possessors of lands or houses sold them and brought the proceeds . . . to the apostles, and distribution was made to each as they had need" (Acts 4:33f.).

Why doesn't Paul *cite* the Jubilee tradition if he is alluding to it? In fact, he does so in the very next verse, which quotes from the story of the wilderness manna (Exod. 16:18). As already noted above in the Preface, this tale provides the foundation for sabbath ideology in the Hebrew Bible, of which the Jubilee is the culminating expression. Not only is the manna a symbol of God's sustaining grace (it is "free"); it also symbolizes the economic principle of *enough for everyone*, which specifically prohibits surplus accumulation (16:19). Indeed the Acts account may well have been inspired by the concluding phrase of Exod. 16:18, which Paul omits from his citiation: "They gathered as much as each of them needed." By rooting his entire appeal to the Corinthians in the story of manna, Paul makes it clear that his reference point is the sabbath economics of grace. Only this can prevent them from acting according to the political economy of patronage and insure that their "gift may be prepared not as 'extortion' but as a 'blessing'" (9:5)

GOSPEL: MARK 5:21-43

We resume Mark's narrative with Jesus' return back to the "Jewish side" of the Sea (v. 21). In the meantime he has brought liberation to the Decapolis in the exorcism of the Gerasene demoniac, a text unfortunately eschewed by all four lectionaries (except as an alternative *BCP* lesson last Sunday). Today's lesson is a remarkable "tale of two women." It is the clearest example of Mark's "sandwich" construction that wraps a story-within-a-story. The purpose of this form is to compel the reader to *relate the two stories to each other*—which is why the lectionaries are missing the point by dividing the text up into one episode or the other. If ever an entire passage should be read, this is it!

The setting of the first half of the story is the "crowd" (vv. 21, 24, 27, 31), which in Mark represents Jesus' social location among the poor. Jesus is approached by a synagogue ruler who appeals on behalf of a daughter he believes to be "at the point of death" (v. 23). Jesus departs with him, and as readers we fully expect this mission to be completed. On his way, however, Jesus is again pressed by the crowds (v. 24). The narrative focus suddenly zooms in upon a woman whose condition Mark describes in uncharacteristic detail with a series of four participial clauses:

> She had been with a flow of blood for twelve years;
>> had suffered much under the care of many doctors;
>> had spent all her resources yet
>> had not benefited but grown worse instead. (vv. 25f.)

According to the purity code a regularly menstruating woman had to be quarantined (see Lev. 15:19ff.), so it would have been highly inappropriate for a woman suffering from unarrestable hemorrhaging to appear in public, much less to approach a "holy man"! But Mark has no interest in purity issues; instead he focuses upon the way that profiteering physicians perpetuate the cycle of sickness and poverty.

The woman's approach to Jesus could not stand in starker contrast to that of Jairus. The latter's approach was frontal and proprietary, acknowledging Jesus' honor by lowering himself in order to make a request. She, on the other hand, reaches out anonymously from behind in the crowd, seeking to touch Jesus covertly and somehow effect a magical cure. There was no impediment to Jairus' petition; the woman's touch causes a stir (v. 31). Even their speech distinguishes them: Jairus addresses Jesus directly, as would befit male equals, while the woman talks only to herself (v. 28). Mark is painting a portrait, in other words, of two characters who represent the opposite ends of the social spectrum. Jairus is the "head" of both his family and the synagogue; the woman is nameless, homeless, childless, and alone.

At the moment of contact between Jesus and this woman (v. 29), however, the power dynamics of this story begin to be reversed. Her body is healed—the opposite of what a Jewish audience would expect, since it is Jesus who should have contracted her impurity through physical contact. Indeed Mark tells us that power had been transferred (v. 30). Is this a magical transaction or a clue to the social reversals to come? When Jesus stops to inquire after the nature of the interruption, the whole narrative, which was in motion toward Jairus' house, grinds to a halt. A struggle ensues between Jesus and the disciples:

Jesus turned in the crowd: "Who touched my clothes?"
Disciples: "You see the crowd yet ask, 'Who touched me?'"
Jesus looked around to see who had done it. (v. 31f.)

To the disciples this is an inconvenience attributable to the crowd, with whom they are unconcerned. Jesus, however, seeks to know the human face of the poor.

It is now the woman's turn to fall in front of Jesus, suggesting that she is now an equal to Jairus (v. 33). As she emerges from the margins of the story to its center she suddenly finds her voice. "She told him the *whole* truth"—including no doubt her opinion of the purity system and the medical establishment that disenfranchised her! Jesus' response is to acknowledge her rightful status as "daughter" in the family of Israel (v. 34). He commends her faith, made evident by her stubborn initiative. This grants her a status *exceeding* that of Jesus' own male disciples, who have been shown to be "without faith" (4:40)!

But what of the original "daughter"? Jairus is informed by some servants that she has died (v. 35). The phrase "while Jesus was still speaking" functions to overlap the two utterances, as if the voicing of gain and loss is simultaneous:

> *Daughter*, your faith has made you well. Go in peace.
> Your *daughter* is dead. Why trouble the teacher further?

In attending to this woman Jesus appears to have defaulted on his original task. Will the story end in tragedy? Undeterred, Jesus ignores this "interpretation" of events and exhorts Jairus to believe. The shock cannot be missed: He is instructing a leader of the synagogue to learn about faith from this outcast woman (v. 36)! The contrast in character is now reversed. Her story is believed; his is not. She has a name ("Daughter!"); Jairus is referred to as "the ruler" (v. 35) and "the child's father" (v. 40).

The scene now shifts to Jairus' household, where mourning turns to derision at Jesus' insistence that the girl only "sleeps" (v. 39). He is not being coy; "being asleep" will emerge later in Mark's Gospel as a symbol of lack of faith (see 13:36; 14:32ff.). Perhaps angry, Jesus throws out the onlookers and proceeds to raise the girl back to life (v. 42). The witnesses are "beside themselves with great astonishment" (v. 43), a reaction that will occur only one other time in Mark: at Jesus' resurrection (see 16:6). Jesus is being portrayed in the tradition of the prophet Elisha, who raised the dead son of a woman of Shunem (see 2 Kings 4:8-37). This may help explain why Mark's story ends with Jesus' strange instruction to give the girl "something to eat" (v. 43). For just as Elisha followed his healing of the young boy by multiplying loaves for people during a famine (see 2 Kings 4:38-44), Mark will shortly narrate Jesus' feeding of the crowds in the wilderness (Mark 6:35ff.).

In narrative interpretation we must assume that every detail is there for a reason, and Mark's apparently innocent aside that the girl was twelve years old (and that the bleeding woman had suffered for the same period) is a good case in point. This shared number invites us now to compare the bleeding woman with Jairus's daughter. The young girl has lived well for twelve years and is coming into puberty where she will begin bleeding, full of fecundity. The old woman has suffered for the same twelve years, barren as the life bleeds out of her. The number also represents the key to the social meaning of this doublet, symbolizing the twelve tribes of Israel (as it did in 3:13). Within the "family" of Israel, Mark contends, one "daughter" represents the privileged, the other the impoverished. Because of such inequity, the body politic of the synagogue is "on the verge of death," something Jairus acknowledges (v. 23a). The healing journey must, however, take a necessary detour that stops to listen to the pain of the crowd. Only when the excluded woman is restored to true daughterhood can the whole body "be made well and live" (v. 23b). *That* is the faith the privileged must learn from the poor. This story thus *shows* what Jesus will later also *tell*: The "last will be first" and the "least will be greatest" (see 10:31, 43).

HOMILETICAL REFLECTIONS

The overwhelming emphasis in the second lesson and the Gospel on economic justice suggests using the *BCP* first lesson for the sermon. In this case the preacher has three powerful elements to weave together:

  a. the Deuteronomic call to seventh-year debt-remission so "there will be no one in need among you" (Deut. 15:4);
  b. Paul's appeal for one church community to act in economic solidarity with another based upon the reality of God's grace, the principle of equality ("from each as they are able") and the manna story's promise of sustenance ("to each as they need");
  c. Mark's dramatization of the way in which the poor were given priority in the ministry of Jesus.

If Pentecost was not occasion for preaching about the Jubilee, this week ought to be. In today's global economic order, in which the poor are being crushed by burdens of debt, the sabbath *still* calls us to debt-remission. In our world, increasingly polarized between the few with surplus and the

many in need, God's grace is *still* "all about equality" (2 Cor. 8:14). And
though we ourselves persist in focusing on the important people in society
while ignoring the outcast, Jesus still takes time to embrace the anony-
mous, the sick, and the exploited.

Admittedly today's themes of redistributive economic justice and
"God's bias toward the poor" are not popular in our churches, so thorough-
ly have we internalized the dictates and the culture of capitalism. But however marginalized these texts have become in North American Christianity,
they are central to the biblical tradition. Paul reminds us that this is the justice *of God* (2 Cor. 5:21), which does not conform to our of traditions of
charity, our structures of class entitlement, or our systems of meritocracy.
And Mark reminds us that social justice is not about guilt-trips but about
our *own* healing. His "tale of two women" shows that the personal and
social health of the "haves" is inextricably connected to the fate of the
"have-nots."

Seventh Sunday after Pentecost
Fourteenth Sunday in Ordinary Time
Proper 9

Lectionary	First Lesson	Psalm	Second Lesson	Gospel
Revised Common	2 Sam. 5:1-5, 9-10 or Ezek. 2:1-5	Psalm 48 or 123	2 Cor. 12:2-10	Mark 6:1-13
Episcopal (BCP)	Ezek. 2:1-7	Psalm 123	2 Cor. 12:2-10	Mark 6:1-6
Roman Catholic	Ezek. 2:2-5	Ps. 123:1-4	2 Cor. 12:7-10	Mark 6:1-6
Lutheran (LBW)	Ezek. 2:1-5	Ps. 143:1-2, 5-8	2 Cor. 12:7-10	Mark 6:1-6

FIRST LESSON: 2 SAMUEL 5:1-10

The recognition of David as sole ruler over Israel begins the narrative of the "united" monarchy. David emerges triumphant in his struggle with the house of Saul, though he is portrayed piously as a "humble winner" who properly refuses to rejoice in the deaths of his political opponents Saul (chap. 1), Abner (chap. 3), and Ishbaal (chap. 4). The consolidation of power is still somewhat ambiguous at this stage, however, since the northern tribes initially speak of Saul as a "king" (Heb. *melek*) and David as a "ruler" (Heb. *nāgîd*; v. 2). Writes Gottwald: "There is a difference of interpretation as to whether David was king over a single political entity Israel, or whether he joined the kingdoms of Israel and Judah in a personal union, mediated by his rule from the independently captured Canaanite city-state of Jerusalem" (1984:320f.). This suggests that the later split between north and south resulted from tensions built into the Israelite State from its inception.

One of David's first moves to consolidate power and cement the alliance was to choose the non-Israelite, fortified city of Jerusalem as a "compromise" political and cultic center, eclipsing the role of Hebron in the south and Shiloh or Shechem in the north (v. 5b). Dozeman uses as an analogy the way in which the newly independent, federated thirteen American colonies settled on a new city, centrally located, for their capital rather than one of the established cities north or south (1993:90).

The portrait of David's conquest of Jerusalem using covert action is brief and uninterested in detail (vv. 6-9). This masks the interesting fact that the city had survived for a long period as an independent Jebusite stronghold, without a king although surrounded by Israelite settlements. Gottwald believes this suggests that Jerusalem enjoyed a "neutral" live-

and-let-live relationship with the tribal confederacy, one that would have been breached by David. This may account for the apparent lack of resistance by the Jebusites on the one hand, and the decision by David to incorporate the city's inhabitants into his administrative center on the other.

Other Lessons: Ezekiel 2:1-7 relates God's instructions to the great prophet-in-exile. They follow upon the vision of the "appearance of the likeness of the glory of the Lord" (1:28) in chap. 1 and precede the command to eat the sweet/bitter scroll (chap. 3). Ezekiel's commission is not unlike Isaiah's (see above, Trinity Sunday). The refrain emphasizes that the prophet's vocation is to speak the hard truth to one's own people regardless of "whether they hear or refuse to hear" (vv. 5, 7). The phrase "though briers and thorns surround you and you live among scorpions" may either be a metaphor for hostility or a more literal allusion to being thrown out into the desert (v. 6). This lesson is more relevant to the themes of the second lesson and Gospel than the 2 Samuel reading.

SECOND LESSON: 2 CORINTHIANS 12:2-10

This is our last week in 2 Corinthians. Today's lesson is taken from what probably is a later correspondence of Paul to that church (see Furnish:29ff.). In this letter Paul is much more explicit in his defense against and criticism of the "rival" group that had attacked the legitimacy of his apostleship than he was in the earlier part of the epistle (see 10:10-12; 11:4-6, 12-15). Furnish believes that this dissident group had so undermined Paul's credibility with the Corinthians that they now refused to go forward with the collection for the Jerusalem church (see last Sunday's second lesson). This would certainly account for the sharper tone in this part of 2 Corinthians. Paul uses a number of rhetorical strategies to regain his church's loyalty, including direct appeals for obedience (10:5f.); answering allegations against him (10:10f.); expressions of jealous love (11:2); attacking his critics (11:12-15); even outright boasting (11:22ff.). In today's lesson, however, he reveals some intimate details of his private life, and even resorts to a little parody of his opponents. This returns us to the essence of his defense: that the only true mark of apostleship is "strength in weakness."

The details of visionary experience Paul alludes to in the thinly veiled third person have been the subject of much pious speculation (12:2-5). Similar descriptions of being "caught up into Paradise" were common in Jewish and Christian apocalyptic literature of that era. But whereas they usually served to introduce "revelations" (see Rev. 1:10ff.), Paul specifically does *not* relate what he saw and heard (v. 4). His strategy is twofold. On one hand, he is answering the apparent accusation that he cannot measure up to his rivals' ecstatic spiritual experiences. On the other, he is parodying the fact that they report on such revelations in order to bolster their status. By saying that "human beings may not utter" what they behold in true visions, Paul is implying that those who *do* talk about it simply haven't been to the "third heaven" (v. 2). He then reiterates his previously articulated position on spiritual gifts (see, e.g., 1 Corinthians 14) by downplaying the usefulness of such private experiences. Paul prefers to be judged on his public service: "What you see and hear is what you get" (v. 6).

But he breaks off this line of defense to become confessional. He has learned humility by enduring a "thorn in the flesh" (vv. 7f.). This oblique reference has fueled still more speculation about the nature of this problem, with theories ranging from sexual temptation to physical or mental ailments. But again the details are not the point; Jesus' assurance to him is (v. 9). "My power is made perfect in weakness" is the thesis statement of Paul's apostolicity. He closes with one more reminder that the true credentials for being an apostle are not elegance and eloquence, but suffering and persecution (v. 10; see 4:8-12; 6:4f.).

Many modern critics of Paul believe he supplanted the praxis-oriented gospel of Jesus of Nazareth with a mystical Christ-religion. I would contend, however, that Paul was every bit as faithful an interpreter of Jesus as, say, the first Gospel writer Mark. Throughout this epistle Paul has insisted that "for the sake of Christ I am content with weaknesses . . . and persecutions, for when I am weak then I am strong" (v. 10). Compare this with Mark's report of Jesus' call to discipleship: "If anyone would come after me, let him deny himself and take up his cross and follow me. For whosoever would save her life will lose it; and whoever loses her life for my sake and the gospel's will save it" (Mark 8:34f.). Do not both voices attest to a Jesus who invites us to the Way of the Cross?

Paul refers to this Way as divine "wisdom"—but acknowledges that to most it will seem like so much "foolishness" (see 1 Cor. 1:18-25). This articulates a genuinely apocalyptic worldview—namely, that ultimate reality is radically discontinuous with the status quo. This is a paradox that religious entrepeneurs, ancient and contemporary, have never fathomed. It was inevitable, then, that Paul would clash with those who were already shaping the gospel to fit conventional religious practices. His opponents vaunted their apostleship through rhetoric, spectacle, and meritocracy, contending for audiences. Paul, however, credentialed his apostleship by "bearing in his body the dying of Jesus" (2 Cor. 4:10), seeking to nurture fellow disciples (11:3f.).

GOSPEL: MARK 6:1-13

At this point in his story Mark slows the narrative pace in order to give us some background on each of the three major "protagonists": Jesus (6:1-6), the disciples (6:7-13, 30), and John the Baptist (6:14-29). The three episodes share a common theme—prophets being rejected—that begins to set the tone for the second half of the Gospel. By weaving these vignettes together Mark implies that all who would preach repentance must reckon with its political consequences, as the story of John's execution makes frighteningly clear.

The series begins with Jesus' return "to his own country" (v. 1). This is the third time he is shown teaching in a synagogue on the sabbath (see 1:21ff.; 3:1ff.), and for a third time he encounters opposition. This time it is not from the authorities, however; it is from the hometown folk. Perhaps jealous of Jesus' notoriety, they are suspicious about his "wisdom" (Gk. *sophia,* only here in Mark) and his work (v. 2). Moreover, they are "scandalized" that this local boy has no distinguished lineage (v. 3), and identify Jesus as "the son of Mary" rather than with his father's family, thus alleging illegitimacy. Sadly, the objections of these small villagers to Jesus' humble origins only reflect their self-contempt (he grew up, after all, among them!). The "prophet without honor" thus makes his final break with the domesticating constraints of household, kinship, and national identity (v. 4; see 3:31-35). Ironically, because of their unbelief they do not get to witness the "powerful deeds" (v. 5f.) that through hearsay they had found so disturbing (v. 2c). Disowned, Jesus moves back into his itinerant mission (v. 6b).

For a second time Mark regenerates the narrative after rejection with a discipleship story:

3:1-6:	Rejection in Capernaum synagogue
3:13-15:	Jesus summons disciples, appoints them to preach and cast out demons
6:1-6:	Rejection in Nazareth synagogue
6:7-13:	Jesus summons disciples, sends them to preach repentance, heal, and cast out demons

The disciples are dispatched with explicit instructions to take only the bare necessities for travel on their mission. In fact, Mark seems more interested in Jesus' ground rules for "the Way" (v. 8) than in the mission itself, which is reported only in summary fashion (v. 12f.). This suggests that these instructions articulate something fundamental for the life of the "apostolic" church (Mark's disciples are called apostles only in v. 30).

The point of this "dress code" is not asceticism, since Jesus has already rejected cosmetic piety (see 2:18-22). Instead it exhorts Christian missionaries to be dependent upon the hospitality of the people they serve. Rendered a stranger at home, Jesus instructs his exilic community to be at home among strangers. The rule of thumb is simple. Where the message of the sovereignty of God is received and embraced, disciples are to remain and build community with their hosts (today we might call this inculturation). Where the message is rejected—and Jesus assumes this will happen—they are to move on with nothing more than a symbolic gesture (v. 10f.). Such a *modus operandus* clearly severs evangelism from any practice of domination or conquest. How different the history of the world since Columbus would have been had Christian missionaries heeded these clear directives!

Intruding between the departure and return of the apostles (v. 30) is the account of John the Baptist's fate at the hands of Herod (next week's lesson). This narrative structure suggests that John's tragic end is part of the missionary instruction. Why does the gospel assume that such persecution is inevitable? The reason lies in v. 12: "They went out and preached that people should repent" (Gk. *metanoōsin*). Vincent Taylor describes this verb as connoting "a deliberate turning, or a coming to one's senses resulting in a change of conduct" (1952:154). This challenge is directed to the people collectively, not only to individuals, and is addressed first and foremost to their leadership in the belief that the entire social project is headed in the wrong historical direction and must fundamentally change course. Public criticism arouses official opposition in a way no private religious counsel could. It is *this* vocation that John passed on to Jesus (see 1:14f.), and that Jesus here passes on to the disciples.

HOMILETICAL REFLECTIONS

The theme of the readings this week is "prophets without honor," or what we might more clearly call "speaking hard truths to one's own people." Since in 1997 this Sunday falls on July 6—in the United States that long holiday weekend of fireworks, historical legend, and national chauvinism—we would do well to ask how the challenge of Ezekiel, Jesus, and Paul speaks to our own situation. Too many North American preachers are too easily "dismayed by looks" (Ezek. 2:6) of disapproval from their congregations, ever concerned about losing market share in the competitive world of religion-as-entertainment. Too few of us can say with Paul that "we will only boast of our own weakness" (2 Cor. 12:5). And all of us compromise the gospel of repentance because we, against Jesus' express instructions, carry too much "baggage."

But repentance is at the heart of biblical faith; take it away and you have something else. The problem is, repentance represents discontinuity with the established order, and for those entitled within it the greatest social value is continuity. From their perspective the system works: it has no fatal contradictions, it perpetuates itself, it even grows and spreads. Substantive notions of repentance, therefore, are necessarily held in contempt—as opposed to spiritualized ones, which are always welcome. Consequently, the theology of conversion—once taken seriously by Protestant immigrants—has become increasingly marginalized in our churches.

The discourse of "changing historical directions" enjoys no hospitality in North America because we are socialized to believe that we are in control of history. And if that faith is shaken, we usually swing over to the other end of the pendulum, abandoning history altogether for private distractions. But recent events, from the Gulf War to the Los Angeles uprising, indicate that we are indeed sowing the seeds of our own demise, facing self-destruction either by our guns or by the gulf between rich and poor. We face a new century in which our exploitation of the earth has resulted in spreading ecological rebellion: drought, aquifer contamination, rain forest destruction, ozone depletion. As Wendell Berry contends, we have become dependent upon what we know is wrong: "We all live by robbing nature, but our standard of living demands that the robbery shall continue" (1989:19ff.).

"Empire," concurs William Appleman Williams, "is the child of an inability or an unwillingness to live within one's own means; empire as a way of life is predicated upon having more than one needs" (1980:31). We have become so internally and externally reliant upon our excesses and appetites that we simply cannot imagine the world differently. We are, in other words, captive in the "land of the free," culpable for both our own dehumanization and that of others, unable to dream of exodus because our own utopian dreams have soured. Our historical project has arrived, whether we have the courage to acknowledge it or not, at a cul-de-sac. The future is closed unless we turn around (see Myers, 1994).

For the prophets of Israel, the call to repentance represented a judgment upon the historical project of Israel, with its illusions of a benign past and an equally benign future. But theirs was a message of solidarity with, not escape from that history, with the hope of reclaiming and redeeming that project. Standing firmly within this tradition were both Jesus and Paul. They each called people to abandon the debt system for the divine economy of grace, in which all good things were "free." And they understood that this freedom "costs us everything" in the real world.

Eighth Sunday after Pentecost
Fifteenth Sunday in Ordinary Time
Proper 10

Lectionary	First Lesson	Psalm	Second Lesson	Gospel
Revised Common	2 Sam. 6:1-5,12b-19 or Amos 7:7-15	Psalm 24 or Ps. 85:8-13	Eph. 1:3-14	Mark 6:14-29
Episcopal (BCP)	Amos 7:7-15	Psalm 85 or 85:7-13	Eph. 1:1-14	Mark 6:7-13
Roman Catholic	Amos 7:12-15	Ps. 85:8-14	Eph. 1:3-14 or 3-10	Mark 6:7-13
Lutheran (LBW)	Amos 7:10-15	Ps. 85:8-13	Eph. 1:3-14	Mark 6:7-13

FIRST LESSON: 2 SAMUEL 6:1-19

The story of the ark's removal to Jerusalem continues the narrative of David's rise to power in 2 Samuel. Our passage begins and concludes with David and the congregation dancing and celebrating before the ark (vv. 5, 14f.), although his triumphant entry into the city spells the end of his stormy relationship with Michal, Saul's daughter (v. 16). The ark is described by Gottwald as

> a wooden chest that appears to have represented the presence of Yahweh in the form of a pedestal or throne for the imageless deity. It is also conceived as a repository for tablets containing the Decalogue. It had a function to accompany the Israelites in battle, serving as a palladium, that is, a sacred object with the power to safeguard those who possessed it. (1984:214)

As a portable shrine the ark symbolized God's journey with the people, distinct from other institutionalized cultic sites. As a cultic war piece it symbolized the conviction that Yahweh, not weaponry, won battles for Israel (see, e.g., 5:19; 8:14).

Interestingly, however, the narrative posits a rather strained relationship between David and the ark. When Uzzah is killed by God for reaching out to steady the ark when it looked as if it might tip over from the cart, David becomes both angry and fearful, and refuses to steward such a dangerous force (vv. 6-10). On the other hand, when he observes that the ark brings blessing to the house of Obed-edom, he covets it again and brings it up to Jerusalem (vv. 11f.). Does David want the Ark only insofar as it serves his ends? Next week's lesson narrates David's desire to aggrandize the ark (himself?) by building an elaborate house for it (7:1ff.). The divine rebuke

of this plan suggests that no king can "control" the shrine of the undomesticated God.

Other Lessons: More to the point of the other Lessons is the Amos text
(Amos 7:7-15). Amos, the first of the "classical" prophets, was active during the reign of Jeroboam II (786–746 B.C.E.). With the Assyrian empire on
the wane, this was a time of relative prosperity and security in the northern
kingdom—and of widespread socioeconomic corruption and exploitation
within Israel, which is the focus of Amos' oracles. Our passage, however,
is about Amos's expulsion from the sanctuary at Bethel for his seditious
judgments against Jeroboam (vv. 10-13). In the sole piece of biographical
narrative in the book, Amos identifies himself as a Judean shepherd who
doubled as a dresser of "sycamore" trees (probably the practice of harvesting native fig trees while grazing flocks).

The account of Amos' expulsion from Jeroboam's court is inserted in
the midst of a series of five visions. In the first two Amos relates that he
was able to intercede for the people successfully (7:1-6). In the third, however, God is taking "measurements" for the destruction of Israel (vv. 7f.), a
theme reiterated in 8:1-3 and 9:1-4. Amaziah assumes that Amos is a
prophet-for-hire who has been sent by rivals in the south to undermine
security in the north, and sends him packing back "to Judah to earn your
bread there" (v. 12). But Amos returns the priest's disdain, emphasizing
that he is no professional seer but an honest laborer who was compelled by
God to speak truth to power (v. 14f.). The passage concludes with Amos
repeating that the king will meet his doom in war—an oracle that, although
it did not come to pass in Jeroboam's lifetime, was soon enough fulfilled as
in 722 B.C.E. Israel went "into exile away from its land" (v. 17).

SECOND LESSON: EPHESIANS 1:3-14

The lectionary moves into the Epistle to the Ephesians for several weeks.
The author of Ephesians, who probably should be regarded as a member of
a "Pauline school," takes on the task of summarizing the social character of
the apostle's theology. The epistle is a treatise on the struggle within salvation history to realize God's great plan of reconciliation, focusing upon the
conflict between Christ's inauguration of peace and the powers' perpetua-
tion of enmity. At the heart of this struggle stands the church, which has
inherited the messianic vocation of peacemaking (see Myers, 1980).

Ephesians is a carefully structured argument in three cycles, each composed as a triad. Each triad begins with a prayer or liturgical reference,
moves into a reflection upon peace within the Christian community (what

we might call the "pastoral task"), and closes with a consideration of what it means to proclaim the vision of reconciliation in a world of enmity (the "prophetic task"):

I. FIRST CYCLE
   A. Liturgy:
      i. Prayer: Enlightenment (1:15-19)
      ii. Confession: Christ over the powers (1:20-23)
   B. Gospel in the Church: Forging Peace
      i. Conversion to the Way (2:1-10)
      ii. The cross and social reconciliation (2:11-22)
   C. Gospel in Mission: Evangelizing the Powers
      i. Paul, apostle in prison (3:1, 13)
      ii. The church proclaims the mystery (3:2-12)

II. SECOND CYCLE
   A. Liturgy:
      i. Prayer: Strength to love (3:14-19)
      ii. Doxology: God's power in us (3:20-21)
   B. Gospel in the Church: Maintaining the Peace
      i. Unity in the body of Christ (4:1-16)
      ii. Conversion to the Way (4:17—5:5)
   C. Gospel in Mission: Prophecy to the Powers
      i. Noncooperation and unmasking (5:6-14)
      ii. Vigilance (5:15-18)

III. THIRD CYCLE
   A. Liturgy:
      i. Praise in song, thanksgiving (5:19-20)
   B. Gospel in the Church: Peace within the Family
      i. Unity in marriage (5:21-33)
      ii. Children and slaves (6:1-9)
   C. Gospel in Mission: Resistance to the Powers
      i. Ends, means, and nonviolent warfare (6:10-17)
      ii. Petition for "ambassador in chains" (6:18-20)

The greeting attributes the letter to the hand of Paul in the tradition of pseudepigraphy, but the attestation "to the saints at Ephesus" is absent in the early manuscripts (v. 1). Most commentators now assume that Ephesians was an early "catholic" epistle meant to circulate among churches throughout the region.

The prologue is a long eulogy that introduces the theme of the letter: the mystery of God's "plan" (vv. 3-14). It is a single, run-on sentence full of rich but repetitive blessing-language, suggesting that it may have been a liturgical benediction. Markus Barth, whose commentary on the epistle is still the best, calls this "theology as doxology" (1974:143). The first part of the benediction praises God for the outpouring of blessing and grace upon those "in Christ" (vv. 3-8). The focus upon the *indicative* character of this "chosenness" (v. 4) is understandable in light of the weighty *imperatives* with which the epistle will close (see, e.g., 6:10ff.).

The "thesis statement" of the epistle is stated in vv. 9-10:

> God has made known to us the mystery of God's will
> —according to God's favor, set forth in Christ
> for the administration of the fullness of time—
> to reunify all things in heaven and on earth under Christ.

The fact that this vision is repeatedly stressed as a "mystery" throughout the epistle (see 3:3-6, 9; 6:19) testifies to the author's realism. Human history has long mocked the hope for the genuine reconciliation of everything. Yet the fact that it is a mystery *revealed* invites and challenges us to be part of this new "administration" entrusted to Messiah. The doxological affirmations of vv. 3-8 remind us to live in solidarity with God's will as "citizens" of this social order (v. 5).

The last part of the benediction introduces a second key theme of Ephesians in the following equation: "we" (v. 12) plus "you" (v. 13) will constitute an "us" (v. 14). The writer is Jewish, which though never stated directly is indicated by phrases such as: "we who first hoped in Messiah" (1:12a) and "the circumcision" (2:11). The audience addressed, on the other hand, are Gentile Christians who have "heard the word of truth . . . and have believed" (1:13). This is clearly expressed in 2:11f.: "Remember that at one time you Gentiles in the flesh, called the uncircumcision . . . were separated from Christ, alienated from the commonwealth of Israel and strangers to the covenants of promise." It is the plan of God to deliver a joint "inheritance" to both Gentiles and Jews (1:14).

This we/you discourse strongly suggests that the epistle was written at a time (late first century?) when Gentiles had become the majority in the church. Apparently they were beginning to marginalize both Jewish Christians and the Jewish roots of the faith. This prompted the writer to simply reverse Paul's argument in Romans: if before the apostle insisted on the right of Gentiles to be equal partners in the faith, now he would insist that they remain in solidarity with Jews who, after all, remain "first" in the salvation history of God. Because this unity is not just spiritual but concretely social in character, deep cultural and political enmities must be overcome by the church. This difficult task is the singular burden of Ephesians, as we shall see next week.

GOSPEL: MARK 6:14-29

The RCL lesson is Mark's flashback account of the execution of John the Baptist (for the other lessons, see last week's comments). This insertion belatedly explains the circumstances surrounding the prophet's arrest back in 1:14. Mark tells us that Herod (that is, Herod Antipas, tetrarch of Galilea and Perea from 4 B.C.E.–39 C.E.) believes that Jesus is John coming back to haunt him (vv. 14-16). Insofar as Jesus took up the Baptist's mission of proclaiming repentance, Herod is not wrong (see by comparison the popular report about Jesus in 8:28). But the disturbing implication for the king is that this mission will not die despite his execution of John. It is to that sordid tale that Mark now suddenly switches in vv. 17ff.

The Jewish historian Josephus, a contemporary of Mark, writes that Herod had to get rid of the Baptist for plainly political reasons—John's preaching was stirring up a popular insurrection:

> Herod had John put to death, though he was a good man and had exhorted the Jews to live righteous lives and to practice justice. . . . When others joined the crowds about John and were aroused greatly by his words, Herod became alarmed. Eloquence that had so great an effect on the people might lead to some form of sedition . . . so Herod decided to be rid of him before his work led to an uprising. . . . (*Antiquities* XVIII, v, 2)

This has led many historical critics to dismiss Mark's account of the king's moral predicament as merely pious legend. But Mark's account is hardly pious!

First, intermarriage was fundamental to the building and consolidation of royal dynasties. This was certainly the case with Herod, who had forged a political alliance through his first marriage with the powerful neighboring Nabatean kingdom. So John's objection that Herod should not marry his brother's wife, and so break this alliance, could scarcely have been *more* political (v. 17). Ironically, Antipas was subsequently defeated by King Aretas of Nabatea, which many Jews interpreted as punishment for his execution of John. Second, the half-Jewish Herodians conformed to Jewish law only when they deemed it politically convenient or expedient. Otherwise they agressively promoted Hellenization, since their provincial power was dependent on the good favor of Rome. This policy was resented by Jewish nationalists. By insisting that Herod be accountable to Torah

(v. 18), then, John was aggravating a volatile issue in the tense atmosphere of neocolonial Palestine.

Mark's portrait of Herodian court intrigue, meanwhile, can only be described as a dark parody, almost a political cartoon (vv. 19-28). The king throws a dinner party for the ruling classes of Galilee—the nobility, the army, and the civic leaders (v. 21). But despite this impressive gathering of political, military, and economic interests, it is a young dancing girl and a drunken oath that finally determines the fate of the Baptist (vv. 22-25). This sardonic caricature of the murderous whims of the powerful—human life is traded to save royal face—stands within the biblical tradition that pits prophets against kings (see, for example, the story of Nathan and David, 2 Samuel 12, and Esther and Ahasuerus, Esther 1–7).

The close of the flashback (v. 29) prefigures the fate of Jesus. On the heels of this, Mark returns to the story of the apostolic mission (v. 30), completing the sandwich begun in v. 12. Mark thus relates all three of the Gospel's protagonists (the Baptist, Jesus, and the disciples) to each other. Later in the story Jesus will tell his disciples that the "Human One" (a.k.a. Jesus) will share the fate of "Elijah" (a.k.a. John), according to the "script" of the prophetic vocation (see 9:11-13). This same destiny also awaits those to whom Jesus passes the torch—disciples will have to reckon with their "day in court" (13:9-11), and in the end with their cross as well (8:34-38).

HOMILETICAL REFLECTIONS

This week's lessons offer two directions for preaching. One is to continue last week's theme of "prophecy without honor" by focusing upon the Amos and Mark readings. As he expels him for daring to speak against the powerful Jeroboam, Amaziah taunts Amos about being a prophet-on-payroll and tells him ominously that Bethel is "the *king's* sanctuary, a temple of the *kingdom*" (v. 13). Amaziah is typical of those in power who see religious activity only as a mercenary tool and who view the cult only as an extension of state power. Both Amos and John the Baptist had the courage to speak out against such hubris.

We saw last week that Mark 6:1-30 knits three stories of "truth and consequences" tightly together, offering a realistic forecast for all who preach repentance. In our time the same presumptive arrogance of the powerful is common—as, for example, when a U.S. president initiated the bombing of Iraq by invoking the divine blessing. The prophetic courage to confront this, however, is rare in our churches. Yet when a group of Catholic Workers—decidedly nonprofessional peace advocates—poured their own blood on Air Force planes equipped with cruise missiles bound for the Gulf War, they were exercising such a prophetic spirit. The fact that they went to jail for more than a year for their trouble is further indication that they stood in the tradition of our readings. The practice of witnessing truth to power should be the rule, not the exception, in a church that stands on the shoulders of Jesus and John and Amos.

The other direction for preaching is to prepare the ground for a series in Ephesians and its vision of the reconciliation of all things (Eph. 1:9f.). It is ironic that although this epistle speaks more straightforwardly about "war" and "peace" than any other piece of New Testament literature, it is rarely heard from in the contemporary debates on these issues. Too long exposited as an ethereal tract concerned solely with the individual believer's mystical union with Christ, Ephesians in fact challenges the community of faith to disengage itself from all the ways that societies institutionalize enmity. As David found out, the biblical God will not be coopted into the service of our historical projects (2 Sam. 6:9), for this God has a plan to reconcile *everything* (Eph. 1:10).

Such a gospel will not be popular, which ties this theme to the first. Ephesians is, after all, penned under the name of an "apostle in chains" (3:1, 13; 6:20). It is testimony to its realism that its argument begins by asserting the "unilateral" cessation of social hostilities between Jew and Gentile (Ephesians 2), yet concludes with a "declaration of war" between a nonviolent church and the powers (Eph. 6:10ff.)! Yet if we have the courage to act in concert with God's "plan" we can legitimately join in the liturgy of trinitarian praise we find in the epistle's prologue.

Ninth Sunday after Pentecost
Sixteenth Sunday in Ordinary Time
Proper 11

Lectionary	First Lesson	Psalm	Second Lesson	Gospel
Revised Common	2 Sam. 7:1-14a or Jer. 23:1-6	Ps. 89:20-37 or Psalm 23	Eph. 2:11-22	Mark 6:30-34, 53-56
Episcopal (BCP)	Isa. 57:14b-21	Ps. 22:22-30	Eph. 2:11-22	Mark 6:30-44
Roman Catholic	Jer. 23:1-6	Psalm 23	Eph. 2:13-18	Mark 6:30-34
Lutheran (LBW)	Jer. 23:1-6	Psalm 23	Eph. 2:13-22	Mark 6:30-34

FIRST LESSON: 2 SAMUEL 7:1-14

The narrative of David's attempt to find a home for the ark in 2 Samuel continues, even though the parallel narrative of 1 Samuel 6 has already demonstrated that the ark "knows its own way home" (1 Sam. 6:8). In 2 Samuel 6 the ark moves from the "house of Abindadab" (6:3) to the "house of Obed-edom" (6:10f.) to the "city of David" (v. 12). But David begins to feel uncomfortable that he lives in a nice house while the ark dwells in a tent (7:1f.; see 5:11). Joel Rosenberg has pointed out that there is considerable irony in the semantic interplay between clan "houses" and the "house" of God (1986:113ff.). After all, the houses of Eli, Samuel, and Saul have risen and fallen in this narrative according to their fidelity to God. Moreover, all is not well in David's household, since his wife Michal scorns the fact that he has brought the ark to the south. Her alienation scuttles the possibility of bringing the "houses" of Saul and David together in peace (6:20f.; see 9:1). And David will take his first fall by invading the "house" of Uriah and Bathsheba (chap. 11).

Nathan, who will later unmask David's murderous adultery (chap. 12), here delivers an oracle from God that is decidedly ambiguous (vv. 4-17). The first part of the message, with its sharp rhetorical questions, repudiates David's pretensions to build God a house (vv. 5-7). This is the wilderness experience speaking, the tradition of exodus liberation and a mobile ark that allows the deity to move among *all* the tribes of Israel (v. 7)! The second part, however, switches to classic covenant language (vv. 8f.), affirming that because Israel is now "planted" in a place, God will also "make for you a house" (vv. 10f.). Rosenburg calls this the "etiological founding moment" of the Israelite Temple-state. But it is *God's* construction project, not David's.

The third part of the oracle (vv. 12-16) announces that it will be David's offspring who will "build a house for my name" (v. 13)—a dramatic divine repudiation of David's pretensions. Rosenburg's summary of the point here is apt:

> The oracle does not place the house of David, so to speak, "beyond good and evil." It operates in YHWH's shelter: "Unless YHWH builds the house, in vain do its builders toil over it" (Ps. 127:1). It is a haunted house—visited by the memory of houses that have fallen, warned by provervial examples of unfulfilled housedom. . . . The harmonious mutuality of divine sheltering and human tabernacling that this creation seems to embody is the product of a unique and unprecedented rapprochement between the house of David, the house of Israel, and the "house" of YHWH. (1986:121)

Other Lessons: The *BCP* lesson (Isa. 57:14-21) is one of Second Isaiah's many promises of restoration to Israel. It portrays a God who dwells both in "high and lofty" places and among the "contrite and humble" (vv. 14f.), who sees Israel's apostasy but vows healing instead of judgment (vv. 16-18). This is God the peacemaker (v. 19), a text that inspires the great hymn to reconciliation in Ephesians 2 (see the second lesson). The *LBW* and Catholic lesson is drawn from Jer. 23:1-6, whose criticism of "shepherds who destroy and scatter the sheep" and promise of the "righteous Branch" connect with today's Gospel lesson.

SECOND LESSON: EPHESIANS 2:11-22

This passage is the theological heart of Ephesians, articulating the concrete historical shape of the cosmic reconciliation in Christ promised in the prologue (see 1:10). Stipulated as a precondition for this new social order, however, is the "turning" of a people from a way of life that "follows" the course of the world and the powers (2:1f.). This conversion is described in consummate Pauline fashion: it is likened to resurrection (vv. 5f.) and is possible only through the "immeasurable wealth of God's grace" (vv. 7f.). Paul's careful dialectic is captured in the claim that the gift of salvation is not "*because* of our works," yet is for the express purpose of *practicing* good works (vv. 8-10). Whenever we have moved from "walking" in debt/sin (v. 2) to "walking" in these good works we represent "God's work of art created in Christ Jesus" (v. 10).

Throughout this epistle the author addresses a community, not just individuals, always using plural pronouns. The argument stands or falls on the creation of a new "people," but this vision is tested upon the historical fact of human enmity, indeed upon a "worst-case" example. In Hellenistic antiquity the cultural, economic, and political conflict between Jew and Gentile was considered to be the prototype of all human hostility. We know from Gal. 1:6-9 that Paul's entire missionary project threatened to founder more than once on this enmity. After reminding the Gentile audience of their alienation from the "commonwealth of Israel" (vv. 12f.), the author begins to attack the ideological foundations of this enmity.

The argument is an extended midrash on Isa. 57:19: "Peace, peace to the far and the near, says the Lord; I will heal my people" (found in today's *BCP* lesson). The author asserts that Isaiah's promise has been realized "in the blood of Christ" (v. 13), and then launches a meditation on the cosmic event of the Cross. Christ embodies that peace because he has:

made us both one,
broken down the dividing wall of hostility
    —in his flesh the enmity,
    the law consisting of commandments in statutes—
made peace by creating in himself one new humanity from the two
and thus *reconciled* both, in one body, to God through the cross
    thereby killing the enmity. (vv. 15f.)

This wall is clearly equated with the enmity that divides Jew and Gentile and that is enforced by "statutory law." Does its dismantling allude to Ezek. 13:14, where a "whitewashed" wall represents the false hopes of those who proclaim peace when there is no peace? Does it refer to the five-foot wall that separated the Outer Court of the Gentiles from the rest of the Jerusalem Temple? After all, Paul had at least once been accused of bringing a Gentile into the Temple (see Acts 21:28f.). The meaning of this demolition metaphor is probably inclusive of these and other connotations, because the scope of Christ's abolition of enmity is cosmic.

The author now returns to the Isaiah allusion (v. 17), for the gospel has become the message of peace (6:15; see Isa. 52:7). The result, stated in almost trinitarian fashion, is that in Christ both groups now "have access in one Spirit to the Father" (v. 18). The doctrine of atonement implied by the order of the assertions here is unambiguous: reconciliation with our social enemies is a *precondition* to reconciliation with God! In his classic little book *The Broken Wall*, Markus Barth writes:

If Christ "is peace," then he is by nature a social, even a political event, which marks the overcoming and ending of barriers however deeply founded and highly constructed. . . . When this peace is deprived of its social national or economic dimensions . . . then Jesus Christ is being flatly denied. (1959:44f.)

Christ's cross represents a unilateral declaration of peace by which Christians must abide. Only then are we truly "seated with Christ in the heavenly places" (2:6), an allusion to Christ's sovereignty over the Powers that perpetuate division (see 1:20-23).

Those who do abide by this peace represent a "third force" in history—the reconciled community of the church (vv. 19-22). This is described in clearly political terms, as the formerly alienated status of Gentiles is reversed:

> 2:12: you are . . . excluded from citizenship (Gk. *politeias*) in Israel and strangers (Gk. *xenoi*) to the covenants of promise.

> 2:19: you are no longer *strangers* (Gk. *xenoi*) and "outside the house" (Gk. *paroikos*), but are "fellow citizens" (Gk. *sumpolitai*) with the saints and "members of the household" (Gk. *oikeioi*) of God.

The writer now moves to an elaborate description of this "house." As Barth puts it, "Those who have been received into God's house are no longer described as its inhabitants in what follows; rather they are declared the building materials" (1984:270). The apostles and prophets are the "foundation" and Christ Jesus the "keystone" (the stone at the top of an arch), the "whole construction fitting together" (vv. 20f.; ibid:314ff.). But only by "building together" can the community become a temple *in* which God dwells, a clear reference to the condition of prior reconciliation between the two alienated peoples (v. 22).

GOSPEL: MARK 6:30-34, 53-56

The division of today's Gospel lesson is inscrutable to me. Why would we read the introduction to the first wilderness feeding but not the feeding itself—particularly when the second feeding is also omitted by the Year B lectionary? And why is the aftermath of the second boat crossing included, but not the voyage itself? I recommend that the preacher include at least the whole of 6:30-44, and my comments will reflect this (see above, the Fifth Sunday after Pentecost).

As soon as the disciples have returned from their first solo mission (see above, the Seventh Sunday after Pentecost), Jesus urges them to withdraw to a wilderness place for reflection (vv. 30-32). But as has been the pattern in Mark, the escape is unsuccessful, for people keep pressing upon them (v. 33; see 1:35-38). Jesus feels "compassion" (Gk. *esplangchnisthē*, literally his "guts were churning") for the crowds and proceeds to teach them until evening (v. 34). The phrase "they were like sheep without a shepherd" recalls Moses' appointment of Joshua as the political-military leader of the tribal confederacy: "May YHWH . . . appoint a leader for this community, to be at their head in all they do, a man who will lead them out and bring them in, so that the community of YHWH may not be like sheep without a shepherd" (Num. 27:16-17). Mark no doubt also means to contrast Jesus with the ruling class of Israel who Ezekiel criticized as "false shepherds":

> Trouble the shepherd of Israel who feed themselves! Shepherds ought to feed their flock, yet you have fed on milk, dressed yourselves in wool and sacrificed the fattest sheep, but failed to feed the flock. You have failed to make weak sheep strong or care for the sick ones or bandage the wounded ones. You have failed to bring back strays or look for the lost. On the contrary, you have ruled them cruelly and violently. (Ezek. 34:2-4)

The prophets Jeremiah (see the other first lesson above) and Zechariah took up this theme as well: "Those who sell them say, 'Blessed be God for I have become rich'; and their own shepherds have no pity on them" (Zech. 11:5). Mark cites a related text later in his passion narrative (Zech. 13:7 = Mark 14:27).

Jesus, on the other hand, is a leader who puts the needs of the poor first. As nightfall approaches at this "wilderness revival," the disciples demand that Jesus send the people away to buy food in the neighboring villages (vv. 35f.). Jesus' response is blunt: "You give them something to eat." The disciples are indignant at the prospect of having to dig into their own pockets to aid the hungry (v. 37). While they agonize, Jesus organizes. Determining the food on hand, he breaks the crowd into groups, says a blessing and distributes the loaves and fish (vv. 38-41). Mark is careful to report that nothing supernatural occurs here, except that "all ate and were satisfied" (v. 42).

This episode makes two other allusions to the Hebrew Scriptures. The most obvious is God's sustaining of hungry Israelites in the wilderness with *manna*, a story that we have seen lies behind the sabbath economics of grace (above, the Preface). But Mark is also drawing upon the "food miracles" of the prophet Elisha during a time of famine (2 Kings 4:42-44). These parallels suggests that the economic dimensions to Jesus' wilderness actions are far more important than "eucharistic" symbolism. This story meant to address the concrete historical situation of the majority of Galilee's rural population. Hunger and poverty were widespread among those disenfranchised by a feudal system of land ownership and by a political economy in which the countryside was bled dry by urban and foreign trading interests. The disciples try to solve the problem of hungry masses by referring it to "market economics"—sending the people to village stores, or counting their change. Jesus had warned against this "measures" system, which served only to widen the gap between the "haves" and "have-nots" (see 4:24f.). Instead he enacts a kind of parable of self-sufficiency through a practice of sharing available resources. The parable of the sower envisioned a harvest of unprecedented yield that would shatter the cycle of poverty in which the indentured peasant was trapped (see 4:8). In the wilderness feedings this hope takes flesh in the "miracle of enough." Mark will later make it clear that the discipleship community must embody this alternative economic model of cooperative consumption in its own life (see 10:28-31).

This episode is followed by the second boat voyage to the "other side" (vv. 45-52), at the end of which the disciples contract "Pharaoh's disease" (v. 52; see 3:5). They do not understand the purpose of the crossing, here equated with "the loaves." Yet Jesus presses on with his healing ministry, bringing his practice of liberation into the very marketplaces he eschewed in the wilderness (vv. 53-56). Soon Mark will be interrogating the reader of his story as to whether *we* understand what these "loaves" represent in the symbolics of the Gospel (see 8:14-21)!

HOMILETICAL REFLECTIONS

The Isaiah lesson is directly cited by the Ephesians passage, and the reading from 2 Samuel relates to its reflections on reconstructing the "house" of God. Ephesians speaks of using those who acknowledge the "peace" forged by Christ as building material for this house (Eph. 2:19-22). Christians who abide in this "unilateral disarmament of the church" cannot by definition also cooperate with any of the myriad social constructions of enmity—gender, class, race, and nation. Does not this gospel call us to renounce whatever aspects of our national and/or cultural identity that perpetuate ideologies of division? And does not this include rethinking *fundamental* assumptions, as was the case with the "law and commandments" for Jews? A good analogical test case for us today might be national borders and the problem of immigration in the United States.

As economic anxieties have persisted through the 1990s, anti-immigrant sentiments have reemerged with a vengeance. "There is an unmistakable pattern to recession in the United States," wrote Jorge Bustamante recently; "When unemployment rises beyond politically acceptable levels, xenophobic sentiments go on the march." The vilification of immigrants as scapegoats has led to a new rash of anti-immigrant bills, hate crimes, and reactionary nativism. This is despite the fact that much of the agricultural wealth of the nation today is still built on the backs of Mexican migrant workers, as is the emerging "underground economy" that supports the service and garment industries. Employer sanctions laws have criminalized undocumented immigrants and their work; already the poorest of the poor, they are now further dehumanized as "illegal aliens." With the unleashing of the border patrol has come gross violations of the human rights of the undocumented. Meanwhile the U.S.–Mexico border—the only place where First and Third World stand adjacent—is being militarized and fortified. Even as the wall symbolizing Cold War hostilities was torn down a new wall is being built along the border, where it symbolizes the fear and loathing of the new war against the poor.

According to Ephesians, such a wall mocks the "structural integrity" of the church. The issue for the Paulinist was "access" to social, cultic, and political space in a world where it was severely restricted (Eph. 2:18). *The wall has been torn down*—What might this mean for us in our world of real division? The sanctuary movement that offered hospitality and solidarity to Central American refugees in the 1980s offers a clue. We can learn from the Civil Rights movement as well, in its refusal to abide by the "law and its statutes" of Jim Crow. What is the implication of Ephesians for the gender wars now raging in our culture, or for the second-class status of gays and lesbians in most churches? What about the social architecture of our cities that still insulates rich from poor and divides whites and people of color by the "thin blue line" of police discrimination and the "thick red line" of economic apartheid? If we are not involved in defying these walls, we are simply not living "in Christ."

If division is driven by the market economy, the only hope we North Americans have to realize "co-citizenship" (Eph. 2:19) with the undocumented and outcast is to rediscover the economics of grace dramatized by the Gospel lesson. There is still "enough for everyone" in our world; the problem is distribution. Jesus reiterated the manna principle of just distribution; can we in the church practice anything less? We have excuses *ad nauseum* as to why full economic justice is impossible, of course. But Jesus' unequivocal retort to the objections of his disciples stands: "*You* feed them" (Mark 6:37).

References and Further Reading

BARTH, MARKUS.
    1974   *Ephesians*. The Anchor Bible. 2 vols. Garden City, N.Y.: Doubleday & Co.

    1959   *The Broken Wall: Studies in Ephesians*. Philadelphia: Judson Press.

BEKER, J. CHRISTIAAN.
    1982   *Paul's Apocalyptic Gospel: The Coming Triumph of God*. Philadelphia: Fortress Press.

BERRY, WENDELL.
    1987   *Home Economics*. San Francisco: North Point Press.

BLENKINSOPP, JOSEPH.
    1983   *A History of Prophecy in Israel: From the Settlement in the Land to the Hellenistic Period*. Philadelphia: Westminster Press.

DOZEMAN, THOMAS, ET AL.
    1993   *Preaching the Revised Common Lectionary (Year B, After Pentecost 1)*. Nashville: Abingdon Press.

ELLUL, JACQUES.
    1991   *Anarchy and Christianity*. Translated by G. Bromiley. Grand Rapids, Mich.: Wm. B. Eerdmans. Pp. 46–55.

ELLIOTT, NEIL.
    1994   *Liberating Paul: The Justice of God and the Politics of the Apostle*. Maryknoll, N.Y: Orbis Books.

FURNISH, VICTOR PAUL.
    1984   *II Corinthians*. Anchor Bible, vol. 32a. Garden City, N.Y.: Doubleday & Co.

GOTTWALD, NORMAN.
    1985   *The Hebrew Bible: A Socio-Literary Introduction*. Philadelphia: Fortress Press.

HOWARD-BROOK, WES.
    1994   *Becoming Children of God: John's Gospel and Radical Discipleship*. Maryknoll, N.Y: Orbis Books.

KELLERMANN, BILL WYLIE.
    1991   *Seasons of Faith and Conscience: Kairos, Confession, Liturgy.* Maryknoll, N.Y: Orbis Books.

MALINA, BRUCE, AND RICHARD ROHRBAUGH.
    1992   *Social-Science Commentary on the Synoptic Gospels.* Philadelphia: Fortress Press.

MANN, THOMAS.
    1988   *The Book of the Torah: The Narrative Integrity of the Pentateuch.* Atlanta: John Knox Press.

MYERS, CHED.
    1994   *Who Will Roll Away the Stone? Discipleship Queries for First World Christians.* Maryknoll, N.Y.: Orbis Books.

    1988   *Binding the Strong Man: A Political Reading of Mark's Story of Jesus.* Maryknoll, N.Y.: Orbis Books.

    1980   "Armed with the Gospel of Peace: The Vision of Ephesians." *Theology News and Notes* (Pasadena, Calif.), March, pp. 17ff.

RINGE, SHARON.
    1985   *Jesus, Liberation, and the Biblical Jubilee.* Overtures to Biblical Theology 19. Philadelphia: Fortress Press.

ROSENBURG, JOEL.
    1986   *King and Kin: Political Allegory in the Hebrew Bible.* Indianapolis: Indiana University Press.

TANNEHILL, ROBERT.
    1990   *The Narrative Unity of Luke-Acts: A Literary Interpretation.* Vol 2. Minneapolis: Fortress Press.

TAYLOR, VINCENT.
    1952   *The Gospel According to Mark.* London: MacMillan.

WALZER, MICHAEL.
    1986   *Exodus and Revolution.* New York: Basic Books.

WILLIAMS, WILLIAM APPLEMAN.
    1980   *Empire as a Way of Life.* New York: Oxford University Press.

YOUNG, FRANCES, AND DAVID FORD.
    1987   *Meaning and Truth in Second Corinthians.* Grand Rapids, Mich.:Wm. B. Eerdmans.